Learning to Use your Computer

Angela Bessant

Heinemann Educational Publishers,
Halley Court, Jordan Hill, Oxford OX2 8EJ
A division of Harcourt Education Ltd

Heinemann is a registered trademark of Harcourt Education Limited

First published 2002
2006 2005 2004 2003
10 9 8 7 6 5 4 3 2

A catalogue record for this book is available from the British Library on request.

ISBN 0 435 45547 8

Cover designed by Big Top

Typeset by Techtype, Abingdon, Oxon

Printed and bound in Great Britain by Thomson Litho Ltd

Please note that the examples of websites suggested in this book were up to
date at the time of writing. It is essential for tutors to preview each site before
using it to ensure that the URL is still accurate and the content is appropriate.
We suggest that tutors bookmark useful sites and consider enabling students to
access them through the school or college intranet.

Acknowlegements
The author and publisher would like to thank the following for permission to
reproduce photographs:
Trevor Clifford page 2; Corbis/David H Wells page 4; Epsom page 4; Anthony
King, Medimage pages 1 and 3.

From the author
I would like to pay particular thanks to Camilla Thomas and Pen Gresford at
Heinemann for all their hard work and useful input at critical stages in the
production of this book. I thank students and colleagues, past and present,
who have taught me so much. Special thanks must go to my family for their
involvement and encouragement.

Screen shots
Screen shots reprinted with the permission from Microsoft Corporation; BBC
page 112; The Natural History Museum, London page 113; Google Inc. pages
117 and 118 and Yahoo! page 118.

It is always interesting to have feedback from readers. Please email or write to
me: angela@bessant.co.uk or Angela Bessant c/o Heinemann.

Contents

Introduction

Whom is the book aimed at?

This book is for absolute beginners to computing – those who have never used a computer before (including those with computer phobia) – and for those who feel that, although they have some knowledge of the basics, they really want to clarify things so that they are more in control and confident.

How is the book structured?

The book is divided into a series of 30 tasks. Each can be attempted at one sitting and at your own pace. They are written in non-technical language with any unfamiliar words explained in plain English. The emphasis is on providing just enough information for you to complete the task without being overwhelmed. There are ample diagrams and screen shots (these show exactly what the computer screen should look like at different steps) to make the tasks as straightforward as possible. There are hints and tips on, for example, shortcuts, solutions to common errors and misconceptions. The emphasis is on confidence-building through practice.

In addition, there are quick reference guides that act as a reminder of how to do things, and practice tasks (when appropriate) for consolidation of skills. There is also a glossary of common terms and acronyms to enable you to 'talk the talk'.

What do I need to use this book?

You will need the items listed below (connected and working). You can check that you have these items by asking the supplier of your computer or by asking a friend/relation/other person who is knowledgeable about computers.

- A PC computer using Windows 98 and Microsoft Office 2000.
- A printer.
- If you want to learn and practise using email and searching the Internet you will need to have an Internet connection and a *browser* (this enables you to *surf the Net*, i.e. look for information) and a *program* (instructions that tell the computer what to do) for sending and receiving email (this book uses Internet Explorer 5 and Outlook Express 5).

But what can a computer do for me?

A computer is a handy tool to have at your disposal to help in completing many ordinary, everyday tasks more efficiently and professionally. At first it may seem that there is much to learn but once you get started (with the aid of this book's gradual approach) you will quickly grasp skills that will enable you to complete tasks, like those listed below, in an efficient and enjoyable way. You may even wonder how you ever managed without a computer!

Step-by-step tasks in this book result in producing:

- a letter and envelope
- a dinner menu
- an agenda for a meeting
- minutes of a meeting
- household budget accounts
- recipe conversion
- a curriculum vitae (CV)
- an inventory of household items.

Other tasks include:

- searching the Internet for information, such as train times, news items or almost anything else
- sending and receiving electronic mail (e-mail)
- setting up your computer exactly as you want it.

After working through this book you will be able to make an informed choice as to whether you want to take your computing skills a step further. This could be done through structured courses and qualifications or self-study. Happy computing!

About this book

Default settings

Default settings are those that are automatically set by the computer when you switch on. In the main, this book uses default settings. It is easy to change settings to suit your own way of working. Instructions on how to change the most common settings are included in the Appendix.

Common terms

Common terms used in each application are introduced as you progress through the tasks.

Getting help

There are quick reference guides at th end of chapters and useful information in the Appendix. In addition, when working with your computer, there is access to a Help menu, or pressing the F1 key will activate help. There is also the Office Assistant. Throughout the book, I have hidden this facility so as not to be distracted from the main objectives. More details of the Office Assistant are found in the Appendix.

Note: There are many ways of performing tasks in Windows 98 and Office 2000 applications, for example via the keyboard, mouse or screen menus. For simplicity, the practical exercises usually demonstrate one method. However, instructions are given for other methods at the end of the chapters or in the Appendix. You can decide which are the best methods for you.

This book uses the word 'key' and not 'type' since key is more often associated with computer keyboards. They mean the same thing.

Chapter 1 Your computer and Windows

This chapter contains five structured tasks. These tasks gently introduce you to your computer and the Windows operating environment. Skills and knowledge acquired here are basic and used in other tasks throughout the book. If you are new to computers (or a little rusty or unsure) it is strongly recommended that you complete these tasks before proceeding.

Task 1 Identifying parts of your computer

You do not need to know how an engine works in order to drive a car. Similarly when using a computer you do not need to know in detail how it works. However it can be useful to know a little bit.

> When you have completed this task you will have learnt:
> - the names of the parts that make up your computer system
> - what each part does
> - some computing words.

1.1 The computer system

With the computer turned off, sit in front of your computer system (sometimes referred to as a *PC* (*personal computer*) and, with the aid of Figure 1.1, identify the following:

- the *system box*
- the *monitor*
- the *keyboard*
- the *mouse*
- the *printer*
- the *modem* (if you have one).

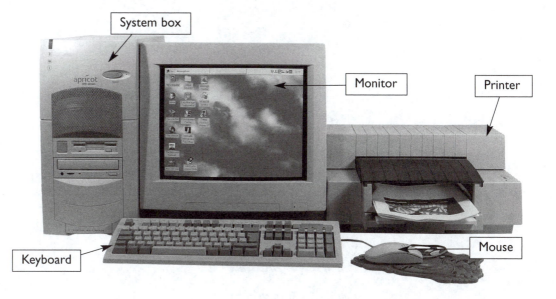

Figure 1.1 A typical computer system

1.2 So what does each of the different parts do?

The system box: on the outside

On the outside of the system box are slots and buttons and there are cables coming from the back, one plugged into the mains electricity socket and the others connected to other parts of the system (Figure 1.2). The slots that you need to know about are the *floppy disk drive* and the *CD (Compact Disk) drive*. Floppy disks and CDs can be used to store information including your own work and also have information stored on them for you to use. They can be removed from the drives and used on other computers. (More about these later.) The button that you need to know about is the *Power* button (to turn the computer on/off).

The system box: on the inside

Inside the system box is the 'brains' of the computer, called the *microprocessor*. It is not intelligent in a general sense but it is extremely accurate, incredibly quick and doesn't get tired! The microprocessor, together with other electronic

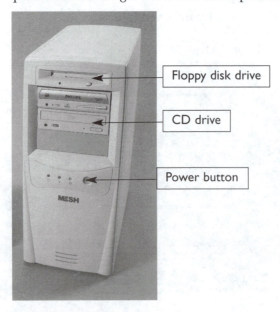

Floppy disk drive

CD drive

Power button

Figure 1.2 The system box

components housed inside the box, carries out sets of instructions. When carrying out instructions and saving results, it needs to store information. It has two main types of storage inside the box. These are a *hard disk* that retains information after the computer is turned off, and *RAM* (Random Access Memory) for temporary storage whilst you are working. The information held in RAM is lost when the computer is turned off.

The monitor

The monitor may look like a television or a flat screen. Its screen displays information and the results of any instructions that you give to the computer. The monitor may have its own mains plug depending on your system.

The keyboard

The keyboard enables you to enter information into the computer. Some people consider using the keyboard to be the same as typewriting. If you can touch-type it will be an advantage but is not essential. When you press the keys on the keyboard, text appears on the screen. If you have used a typewriter you will notice that the main keys are laid out in the same way as a typewriter (see Figure 1.3), i.e. the standard QWERTY layout (QWERTY refers to the first six keys of the top row of letters). The keyboard has some extra keys on it, such as the *function* keys F1, F2 and so on, and the *Ctrl* and *Alt* keys. These are used to perform various tasks and you will learn about these as you progress through the book.

The mouse

The mouse enables you to give instructions to the computer. Using this you can point at things on the screen, select them and move them around. A common mouse has two *buttons*, known as the left button and the right button (Figure 1.4). You need to *click* on one of these buttons at the appropriate time to carry out tasks. When you move the mouse along on your desk (usually it sits on a *mouse mat*) the mouse *pointer* moves on the screen in the same direction.

Figure 1.3 The keyboard

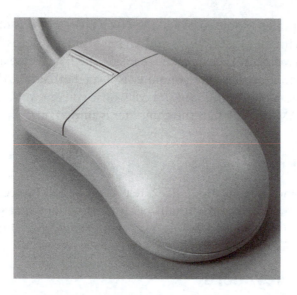

Figure 1.4 The mouse

The printer

There are several different types of printer. Figures 1.5 and 1.6 show two common types. They all have the same purpose in that you load them with paper and when the computer is given instructions to print, the printer responds and prints out the item you have requested so that you have a paper copy (*hard copy*).

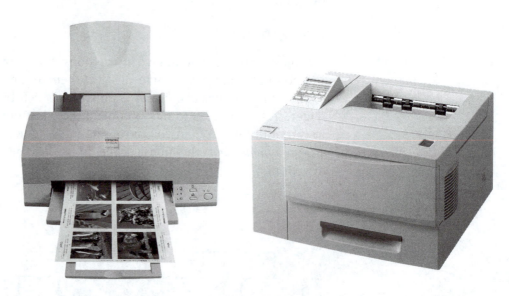

Figure 1.5 Inkjet printer   *Figure 1.6 Laser printer*

Information

The two main types of printer commonly in use are *inkjet* and *laser*. Both inkjets and lasers are quiet in operation and print to a high quality. Lasers are generally quicker and produce the highest-quality output. All types have models available to print in black and white and/or colour. Printers come with a recommendation for types of paper, since the quality of paper used has an effect on the quality of output produced. You can choose a specific paper size from the selection available in the software application. A4 is the most common size.

The modem (if you have one)

If you are connected to the *Internet*, you may see a modem. You may not be able to see this since it might be inside the system box (i.e. an internal modem as opposed to an external one). The modem normally connects to the domestic phone line. It converts data from the computer to a form that can be used by the phone line and vice versa. This enables communication between computers.

Task 2 Are you sitting comfortably?

When driving a car, mowing the lawn or lifting something, it is important that you perform these tasks correctly in order to avoid muscle strains and other injuries. When watching TV, it is sensible to reduce glare on the screen by drawing the curtains or repositioning lighting, and not to sit too close or too far away. Similarly when working with computers, it is worth giving some thought to how best to create a comfortable working environment.

> When you have completed this task you will have learnt:
> - how to reduce any discomfort associated with computer use
> - some more computer words.

2.1 Health and safety

When you are using a computer for prolonged periods it is important that you make yourself comfortable, otherwise you may become easily fatigued or ill. Computing environments in the workplace must conform to the *Health and Safety at Work (HASAW)* legislation. An employer is responsible for providing a safe and comfortable working environment. *Repetitive strain injury (RSI)*, an injury arising from making awkward movements or the prolonged use of particular muscles, is a recognised condition. Eyestrain and headaches have also been linked with working with computers. If this sounds alarming, don't worry! You can eliminate risks by being aware of the information below.

2.2 Eliminating risks

Positioning of the screen	All screens should be adjustable so that you can set them up for your own requirements to avoid muscle strain in the neck and shoulders. The screen should be directly in front of you, roughly at arm's length. The top of the screen display should be just above eye level.
Positioning of documents	To prevent visual fatigue and muscle tension and to minimise re-focusing and twisting the neck, documents should be near the screen, at the same height and distance. Document holders that clip on to the side of the monitor are useful.

Positioning of keyboard	If your keyboard is not comfortable (i.e. it is placed too near the edge of the desk or is too far away to be comfortable), you could put unnecessary strain on your wrists and cause RSI. Keep your wrists straight and try not to bend them upwards when keying in. Wrist rests are available.
Using the mouse	Ensure that you are using the mouse correctly. Keep it in a comfortable position and rest your fingers lightly on the buttons. Do not grip it too tightly or for prolonged periods.
Type of chair	An adjustable chair is essential. Your back should be straight and your feet should rest on the floor. Your forearms should be roughly horizontal when using the keyboard.
Lighting	Screen glare should be avoided by adjusting background lighting and using window blinds or positioning the screen so that it is unaffected. Optional anti-glare filters for screens are available.
Ventilation	Ensure that there is adequate ventilation in your working area.
Frequent breaks	When working at the computer for prolonged periods, it is important to take frequent breaks (about ten minutes every hour) to stretch and walk around. Also, give your eyes a rest so that they do not become tired and sore from staring intently at the small screen area. Focus them in the distance. Consider the possibility that spectacles may be helpful even if you do not normally wear them for reading.
Ensure equipment is safe	It is important to have equipment checked periodically to ensure that it is safe to use. Power cables should be secured so that they cannot be tripped over and power sockets should not be overloaded. Any cable damage should be repaired. Surge protectors can be purchased to protect equipment (particularly modems) from damage during thunderstorms.

Look after your computer	Do not eat and drink while using your computer. Crumbs can become lodged in the keyboard and spilt drinks can cause quite serious damage. Do not pile things on top of the monitor, system box or printer as this could block air vents. Computers should not be moved when they are in use since this may cause damage to the hard disk.

Task 3 Switching on/off and the desktop

This task gets you started on making the computer work for you. Many people feel quite nervous when they use a computer for the first time. Don't worry, computers are very robust in normal use so it is extremely unlikely that you will damage it in any way.

When you have completed this task you will have learnt how to:
- switch the computer on
- identify common things that appear on the screen
- make selections using the mouse
- shut down the computer.

3.1 Switching on the computer

METHOD

1 Ensure that the computer (and monitor if it has a mains cable) is plugged into the electricity mains socket.

2 Press the **Power** button on the computer system box (and on the monitor if it has a separate button) to switch the power on.

3 The computer will perform its start-up checks – i.e. it will make noises and text will appear on and scroll up the screen, and it will load *Windows* (see below). This is sometimes called *powering up* or *booting up*. After a few moments you will see the Windows 98 *desktop* displayed. The items that appear on this screen depend on how your computer is set up. It will look similar to Figure 1.7.

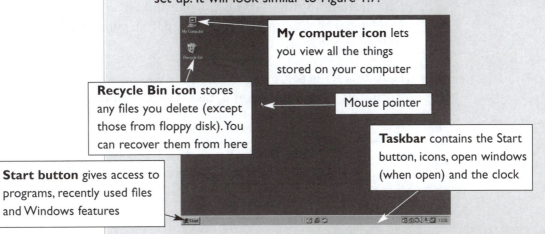

My computer icon lets you view all the things stored on your computer

Recycle Bin icon stores any files you delete (except those from floppy disk). You can recover them from here

Mouse pointer

Taskbar contains the Start button, icons, open windows (when open) and the clock

Start button gives access to programs, recently used files and Windows features

Figure 1.7 Windows 98 desktop

Information

Using passwords

If you are using a password-protected computer, you will need to find out what the procedure is to *login* (i.e. connect you), and what user name and password you should use. Typically something like the boxes shown below appear on your screen.

If you choose/change your own password, you should use something that you will remember, but at the same time something that is not easy for anyone else to guess. Your password may be restricted to a certain number of characters. When you enter your password, it will appear in a form similar to that shown below so that no one can take a sneaky look at it. You will be asked to confirm your password by keying it in again. This ensures that you keyed it in correctly the first time.

Information

In order for the computer to do a useful job, it needs to be instructed what to do. *Software* is the name given to the *programs*, each made up of a series of instructions that tell the computer what to do. There are different types of software: *operating system software* and *applications software*. The operating system software runs the computer and is used to load and run applications software. *Windows* is Microsoft's popular operating system software. Windows makes for relatively easy learning because you don't have to remember complicated commands. It has a **g**raphical **u**ser **i**nterface (*GUI* for short, pronounced 'gooey'), i.e. you click on *buttons* and *icons* (small pictures) to operate the computer.

Word processing, *spreadsheet*, *database* and *drawing programs* are all examples of applications software. *Microsoft Office* and *WordPerfect Office* are examples of integrated applications software. They have popular applications bundled together in one *suite*.

The *desktop* is the first thing you see on your screen when Windows has loaded. You can put things on it, take things off and move things around to suit your way of working (a bit like you would on a normal desk) (Figure 1.7).

3.2 Identifying desktop objects

Using Figure 1.7 locate the following on your desktop:

- Start button
- Taskbar
- Clock
- Recycle Bin icon
- Mouse pointer

Information

Common terms that you need to know that are associated with Windows:

- *Icon* – a small picture that represents an object (e.g. the Recycle Bin icon in Figure 1.7).
- *Button* – using the mouse you click on a button on screen to select an action.
- *Menu* – a list of commands from which you can choose.
- *Dialogue box* – a box that is displayed asking you for information.

Mouse terms:
- *Click* – press and release the left mouse button.
- *Right-click* – press and release the right mouse button.
- *Double-click* – press and release the left mouse button twice rapidly.
- *Drag and drop* – when the mouse pointer is over an object on your screen, press and hold down the left mouse button. Still holding down the button, move to where you want to replace the object. Release the mouse button.
- *Hover* – place the mouse pointer over an object for a few seconds so that something happens – e.g. another menu appears or a *ToolTip* (a message that pops up to advise what the tool does) is displayed.

3.3 Shutting down the computer

METHOD

I   Click on: the **Start** button. The **Start** menu appears (Figure 1.8).

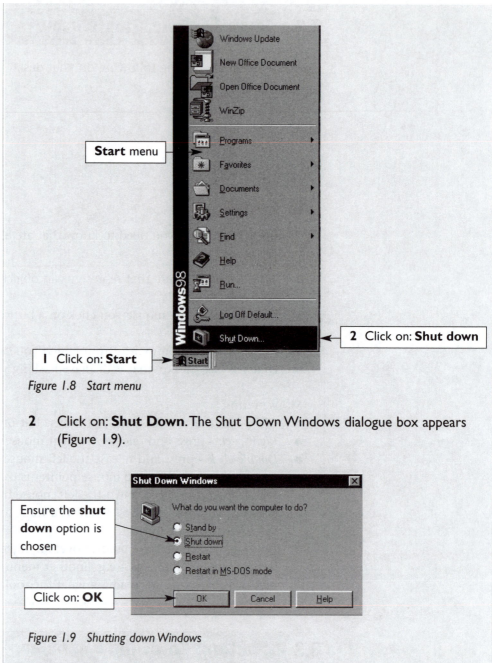

Start menu

1 Click on: **Start**

2 Click on: **Shut down**

Figure 1.8 Start menu

2 Click on: **Shut Down**. The Shut Down Windows dialogue box appears (Figure 1.9).

Ensure the **shut down** option is chosen

Click on: **OK**

Figure 1.9 Shutting down Windows

3 Ensure that there is a dot in the option button next to **Shut down**. If not, click in the button so that a dot is displayed.
4 Click on: **OK**.
5 A message 'It's now safe to turn off your computer' is displayed. Your computer may then switch off automatically. If not, you can now use the power switch to turn off.

Information

It is important that you shut down Windows correctly when you have finished using your computer. If not, files may become corrupted (i.e. there may be damage to data, which might result in you not being able to access your saved work or software). If you have any work that you have not saved, you will be asked if you want to save before shutting down. Any work that has not been saved will be lost when the computer is switched off.

Task 3 Check

Are you familiar with the following?

Starting the computer	
Recognising objects on the desktop	
Shutting down the computer	

Task 4 Mouse skills and Windows

This task provides practice in using the mouse and, at the same time, familiarises you with working with *Windows*. Playing a computerised version of **Solitaire**, the well-known card game, is an excellent and fun way to acquire these skills.

Note: You may find it quite difficult clicking and double-clicking the mouse at first. After a while you should find this easy to do. For some people changing the mouse properties (i.e. slowing it down, changing to left-handed) is helpful.

When you have completed this task you will have learnt how to:
● load a program
● use the mouse
● understand windows
● access Help.

4.1 Loading Solitaire

Information

'Load' is the word used to start or open a program or document.

METHOD

1 Switch the computer on and wait until the Windows desktop appears on screen.
2 Click on: the **Start** button.
3 On the **Start** menu, move the mouse pointer up to **Programs** so that it is highlighted (Figure 1.10).

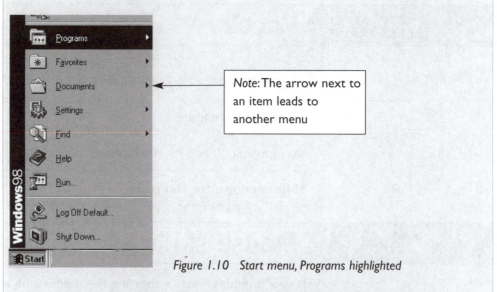

Note: The arrow next to an item leads to another menu

Figure 1.10   Start menu, Programs highlighted

4   A menu automatically appears next to the **Start** menu.
5   Move the mouse across to this menu so that **Accessories** is highlighted.
6   Another menu automatically appears.
7   Move the mouse across this menu so that **Games** is highlighted.
8   Yet another menu appears.
9   Move the mouse to **Solitaire** so that it is highlighted and click the left mouse button.
10 The Solitaire window appears (Figure 1.11). Notice that the taskbar now displays a button for Solitaire (Figure 1.12).

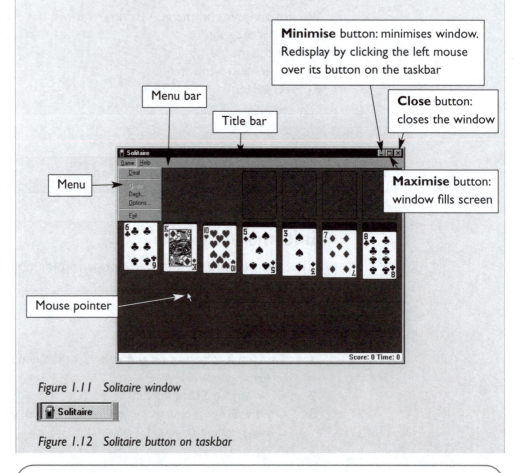

Minimise button: minimises window. Redisplay by clicking the left mouse over its button on the taskbar

Menu bar

Title bar

Close button: closes the window

Menu

Maximise button: window fills screen

Mouse pointer

Figure 1.11   Solitaire window

Figure 1.12   Solitaire button on taskbar

Information

If you do not have **Solitaire** on your computer, **Paint** is another excellent **Accessories** program for practising some of the skills shown below.

Information

Windows is so named because it displays programs or information on screen in rectangular *windows*. Figure 1.11 has labels for the different parts of a window. Note the following:

Title bar – this shows the name of the application being used (i.e. **Solitaire**).

Menu bar – this has menu names that can be selected using the mouse/keyboard. A *drop-down menu* then gives you options within that menu. A drop-down menu (sometimes known as a *pull-down* menu) is displayed from the top of the screen downward when it is selected.

4.2 Accessing Solitaire Help

METHOD

1 On the **Menu** bar, click on: **Help**; a menu appears.
2 Click on: **Help Topics**; the Solitaire Help window appears (Figure 1.13).
3 Click on: the **Contents** tab, if not already selected (on top of **Index** and **Search** tabs).
4 Click on: **Playing Solitaire**.

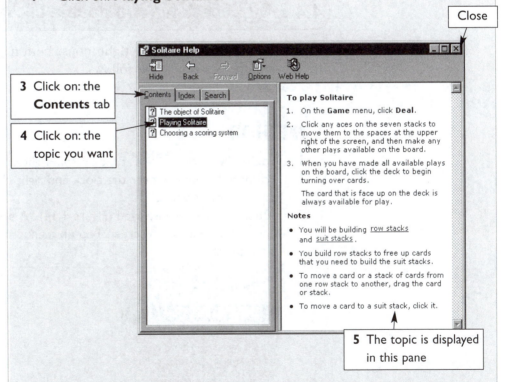

Figure 1.13   Solitaire Help window

5 The rules of the game are displayed in the right-hand pane of the window.
6 When you have read the rules, click on: the **Close** button of the Solitaire Help window (Figure 1.13).

Note: Tabs (as in step 3) are common in Windows. Clicking on a tab reveals contents relating to the tab.

4.3 Playing Solitaire

Congratulations! You are now ready to play Solitaire.

Practice 1

- The mouse actions whilst playing the game.
- Using the menus to get Help and choose other options for the game.
- Moving the window by pointing to the Title bar and dragging and dropping.
- Resizing the window by moving the mouse pointer over the edge of the window until a double-headed arrow appears. Press and hold down the left mouse and drag to the required shape. Release the mouse.

Note: To keep the same proportions of the window, drag from a corner.

When you have had enough practising and want to stop playing, from the **Game** menu, select: **Exit** or click on: the **Close** button.

Note: You can have more than one window open at a time so the skills of moving and resizing them are very useful.

4.4 Right-clicking and double-clicking

In order to practise clicking the right mouse button (i.e. right-clicking), open the clock properties window as follows.

METHOD

1 Locate the clock 14:14 at the bottom right of the taskbar.
2 Position the pointer over the clock and right-click (i.e. click the right mouse button once).
3 A pop-up menu is displayed (Figure 1.14). (A pop-up menu is so called because it pops up on screen. Pop-up menus are usually activated using a right-click.)

Figure 1.14 Pop-up menu

4 Select: **Adjust Date/Time**. The Date/Time Properties box is displayed (Figure 1.15).

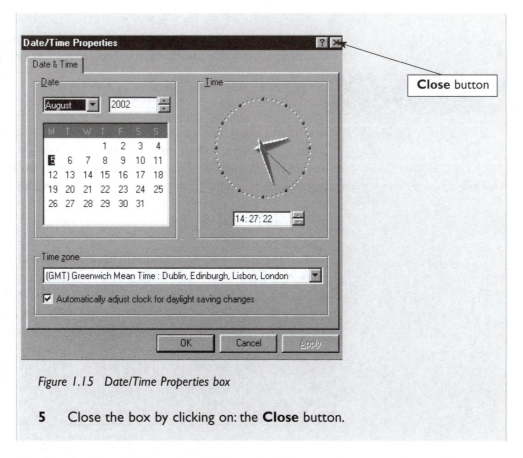

Figure 1.15   Date/Time Properties box

5   Close the box by clicking on: the **Close** button.

Practise double-clicking – i.e. clicking the left mouse button twice rapidly.

METHOD

1   Position the pointer over the clock and double-click (i.e. click the left mouse button twice rapidly).

2   The Date/Time Properties box is displayed (as above).

3   Close the box as above.

Information

You may find double-clicking quite difficult at first. If nothing happens when you double-click, it may be that you are leaving too long a gap between clicks. Keep trying and you will master it.

Task 4 Check

 Are you familiar with the following?

Loading a program	
Using the mouse	
Recognising parts of an application window	
Resizing, rescaling and closing a window	
Moving windows on a desktop	
Accessing Help within a program	
Exiting a program	

Note: You may want to continue practising skills using the program **Paint**. This is accessed from the **Start** menu, **Programs**, **Accessories**, **Paint**.

Task 5 Getting Windows Help

You have already come across using Help when playing Solitaire but the help given was specific to Solitaire (i.e. the application you were using). When working in Windows you can access **Windows Help**. This help is specific to the Windows environment in general. Accessing any help menu is very useful if you have forgotten how to do something or if you want to discover how to do something that you haven't already learnt.

Note: It is sometimes quite difficult to find the help you require using Help menus. Many people prefer using books or asking others for help. To aid searching, try to use specific words that are associated with exactly what you are looking for help with. Sometimes the help is not of much use (especially to a beginner) because it contains so many jargon words or phrases.

When you have completed this task you will have learnt how to:
- access and use Help
- use scroll bars.

5.1 Accessing Windows Help

METHOD

Practise getting help with a topic from Windows 98 Help as follows:

1   From the Windows desktop, click on: **Start**, then on: **Help**. The Windows Help window appears (Figure 1.16).
2   Click on: the **Index** tab.

> 4 The topic will appear here. Double-click on the topic or click on: the topic and then on: **Display**

> 2 Click on: the **Index** tab, if not already selected

> 3 Click in this box and key in the name of the topic you are looking for. In this exercise, key in: date (case does not matter)

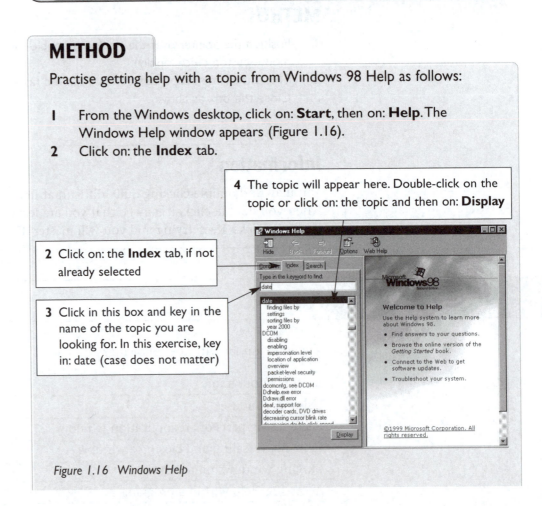

Figure 1.16 Windows Help

3   Click in: the **Type in the keyword to find** box and key in (in this example): **date**.

4   The topic will appear in the box below. Double-click on the topic or click on the topic and then on: **Display**.

5   The Topics Found box appears (Figure 1.17). A list of date-related topics is given.

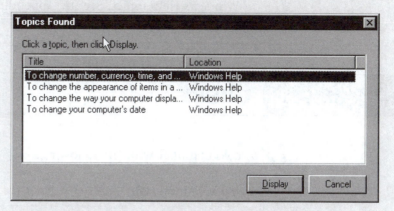

Figure 1.17   Topics Found

6   Choose a topic by clicking on it, then on: **Display**. The example chosen here is 'To change your computer's date' and the Windows Help appears displaying the topic advice in the right-hand pane (Figure 1.18).

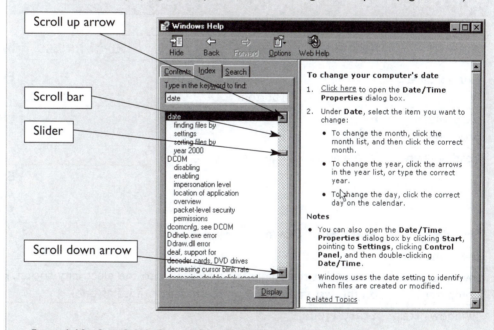

Figure 1.18   Specific Windows Help is displayed

Scroll bars

When a window is not big enough to display all the information in it, scroll bars appear, vertically and/or horizontally (Figure 1.18).

Practice 2

● Clicking on the scroll bar arrows to move through the index entries.
● Dragging the slider along the scroll bar to move more quickly through the entries.
● Searching for other Help topics.

When you have finished searching for Help topics, close the Windows Help window by clicking on: the **Close** button. Shut down the computer as in Task 3.

Information

You can also access Help by pressing: the **F1** key. You can make a printout of Windows Help topics. See the Appendix for instructions of how to do this.

Task 5 **Check**

✓ Are you familiar with the following?

Using Windows Help	
Scroll bars	

Quick Reference: Your computer and Windows

Action	Keyboard	Mouse	Right-mouse	Menu
Exit Solitaire		Click: the ☒ **Close** button		**File**, **Close**
Help within programs	**F1**			**Help**
Load Solitaire	In Windows 98 desktop			
				Start, **Programs**, **Accessories**, **Games**, **Solitaire**
Shut down the computer	**Start, Shut Down**			
Switch on the computer	Ensure that the computer is plugged into the electricity socket. Press the power button on the system box and on the monitor (if it has one)			
Windows Help	**Start, Help**			

Chapter 2 Word processing

This chapter has six tasks for you to try. Tasks 6, 7 and 8 contain many of the basics of using a word processor so it is advisable to attempt these before moving on to any of the others. Since practice makes perfect, you might want to consolidate your skills by completing the optional practice checks at the end of these tasks. Tasks 9, 10 and 11 take you through additional skills required to produce some common documents.

Task 6 First steps in word processing

This task will get you started in word processing, from using the keyboard through to printing a document. You will find the Windows skills learnt in Chapter 1 will be invaluable for enabling swift and sure progress.

When you have completed this task you will have learnt how to:
- know when and why to use a word processor
- load Word
- use the keyboard
- key in some text, numbers and symbols
- save a document
- print a document
- close a document
- exit Word.

6.1 About word processors

Word processing is the most commonly used computer software application. It is very useful because it allows you to create documents, such as letters, advertisements and posters, by keying in text and manipulating documents on screen. You can easily correct any mistakes you make so there's no need to search for an eraser or correction fluid! Documents can be saved as files and printed. These documents can be stored on disk so that they can be recalled and edited at a later date or reused as part of other documents.

Microsoft Word is a word processing application. It has many powerful features compared with the most elaborate typewriter. These include *formatting* – i.e. changing the appearance of text (e.g. its size, appearance and position); checking spelling; creating indexes; and handling graphics. In fact you have a great deal of control over the look of your final document. You will learn more about some of these features as you progress through this chapter. Once the basics have been learnt, it is easy to produce professional-looking documents.

6.2 Loading Word

METHOD

1. Switch on your computer and wait until the Windows 98 desktop screen appears.
2. Move the mouse cursor over the **Start** button and click the left button – the **Start** menu appears.
3. Select: **Programs** by moving the mouse over it – another menu appears.
4. Select: **Microsoft Word** and click the left button (Figure 2.1).

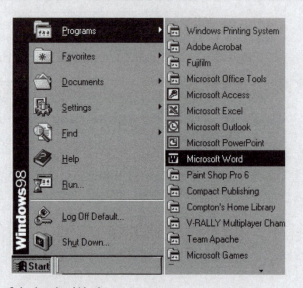

Figure 2.1   Loading Word

Information

If you have a shortcut icon to Word on your desktop, you can load Word by clicking or double-clicking on: the ▦ **Word** icon.

The Word Document window is displayed on screen (Figure 2.2) showing a new blank document with *default* values (i.e. settings that are automatically used, such as line spacing and width of margins). These settings will remain unchanged unless you alter them.

Information

If there is no Document window, click on: the ▯ **New** button at the top left of the toolbar

or

Select: **New** from the **File** menu; the **New** window will appear. Click on: the **General** tab, **Blank Document** and **OK**.

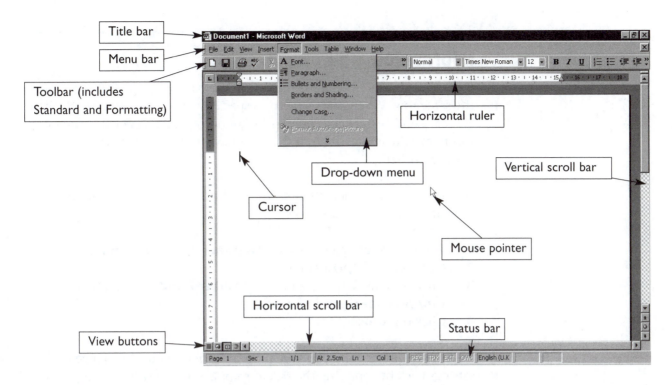

Title bar

Menu bar

Toolbar (includes Standard and Formatting)

Horizontal ruler

Drop-down menu

Vertical scroll bar

Cursor

Mouse pointer

Horizontal scroll bar

Status bar

View buttons

Figure 2.2   The Word Document window

6.3 Parts of the document window – an overview

Title bar

This shows the current document name, **Document1** (this is the default name) and the name of the application being used, Microsoft Word.

Menu bar

This has menu names that can be selected using the mouse/keyboard. A *drop-down menu* then gives you options within that menu. This initially displays options used most recently. After a few seconds, the drop-down menu expands to include all available options. These menus will personalise to display your most recently selected options as you progress through your work.

Standard toolbar

This contains shortcut buttons for actions used frequently. For example, to print a document, click on: the **Print** button shown in Figure 2.3.

Print

Figure 2.3   Standard toolbar button Print

To find out quickly what each button on the toolbar does, hover the mouse over the button and wait for a few seconds. A *ToolTip* will appear giving a brief explanation of the button. Try this now.

Formatting toolbar

This allows shortcuts to formatting your document, such as underlining text or centring text.

Information

By default the Standard and Formatting toolbars are displayed together on the same row. When practising it is especially useful to display both the Standard and Formatting toolbars in full on separate rows (the exercises in this book will assume this) so that you have all the buttons that you can click on in sight.

To change from the default and display the Standard and Formatting toolbars in full on separate rows:

1   From the **View** menu, select: **Toolbars**, then: **Customize**.
2   Click on: the **Options** tab.
3   Click to remove the tick in the **Standard and Formatting toolbars share one row** box.
4   Click on: **Close**.

Note: If you prefer, when you are more proficient, you can change the settings back by replacing the tick at step 3. You will still have access to the remaining options on each toolbar by clicking on: the ⟩⟩ **More Buttons** button.

Cursor	The cursor flashes where your text will appear.
Horizontal ruler	This shows the position of text and can be displayed in centimetres or inches. (See the Appendix to change the default.)
Mouse pointer	This will move when you move the mouse – use to select items in the window. The mouse pointer changes shape depending on where it is on the screen.
Scroll bars	You can scroll quickly through your document using the scroll bars.
Status bar	This provides information about the position of the cursor and the text displayed on your screen.
View buttons	There are different ways of viewing your text. This book uses **Normal View** (the furthest left of the View buttons). Click on this now. This view allows fast editing. (See the Appendix for more information on types of View.)

6.4   The keyboard

Before keying anything in to Word, take some time to have a close look at the keyboard. Most keyboards are quite similar so it will look something like Figure 2.4. Those who have used typewriters will recognise the standard QWERTY keyboard layout (QWERTY refers to the first six letters on the top row). A computer keyboard has extra keys.

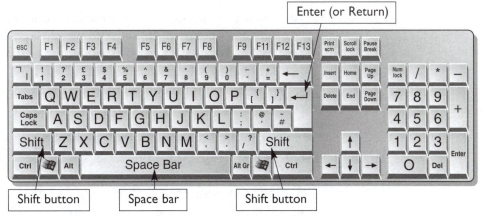

Figure 2.4 Keyboard layout

The extra keys that you need to know about at this stage are labelled in Figure 2.4. They include the following.

Shift

There are two **Shift** keys, one at either side of the character keys. They perform the same task so you can use whichever is most convenient. Using the **Shift** key produces uppercase (capital) letters. Press the **Shift** key down at the same time as the character key – i.e. holding down **Shift** and pressing **R** produces uppercase **R**.

Some keys have two characters (e.g. the number keys above the QWERTY row). For instance, the number 1 key also has an exclamation mark (!), the number 5 key, a % symbol. To produce the character shown on the upper part of these keys, hold down the **Shift** key and at the same time press the required key.

Enter (or Return)

When the text is too long to fit within the space available, it will automatically be carried over to the next line. This is known as *word wrap*. However, if you have not reached the end of a line but want to move to the next line, you need to press the **Enter** key. If you want to leave a blank line, say after headings or between paragraphs, press the **Enter** key twice.

Space bar

Use the space bar to create a space in between words. Try to be consistent. One space after a comma and one space (or two) after a full stop is acceptable, looks neat and is easy to read.

Information

- Depending on your default settings, you may notice red or green wavy lines appearing under text as you key in. You need not be concerned about these for now. They are addressed in Task 7.
- You can check that you have been consistent with spacing by clicking on: the ¶ **Show/Hide** button. This displays spaces as dots. Therefore a space appears as one dot. To turn **Show/Hide** off, click on: the **Show/Hide** button again.

- If you are keying in a block of capital letters, press: the **Caps Lock** key to start keying in capitals and press: **Caps Lock** again to stop.
- Many keys have a 'toggle' function (i.e. they change selection each time they are pressed).

  For more information on layout, see the appendix.

6.5 Keying in text

Key in the following letters (at this stage do not worry if you make mistakes, you will learn how to correct them later):

qwerty

Leave a space (press the space bar once) and key in the same, this time in uppercase (i.e. capital letters):

QWERTY

Move to the next line by pressing: **Enter**.

The keyed in text will look similar to Figure 2.5. Notice how the *cursor* moves with you as you key in.

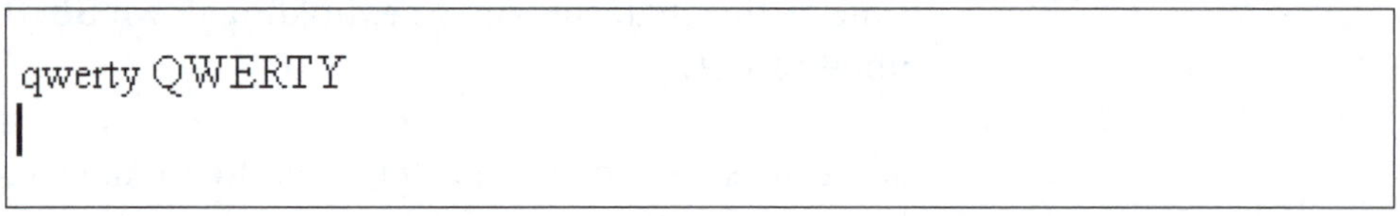

qwerty QWERTY

Figure 2.5 Text keyed in

6.6 Using all the letters of the alphabet

Key in the following:

The quick brown fox jumps over the lazy dog.

6.7 Creating line spaces

Leave a line space by pressing: **Enter** twice and key in your name.

6.8 Keying in numbers and symbols

Leave a line space and key in the following numbers and symbols. Leave a space between each one.

2 ! 4 = 1 / & 3 – 8 # 6 @ 7 : 5 ? £ % * + , 9

Results of your keying in will now look like Figure 2.6.

```
qwerty QWERTY
The quick brown fox jumps over the lazy dog.

[Your name]

2 ! 4 = 1 / & 3 − 8 # 6 @ 7 : 5 ? £ % * + , 9
|
```

Figure 2.6   More keying in

6.9   Saving a document

Information

The great thing about using a word processor is that you can save your work so that you can recall it at a later date to make alterations, update it, use it (or parts of it) in another document, print it and so on. Note that the document, when saved, is referred to as a *file*. When working on documents it is good practice to save your work at regular intervals just in case something goes wrong with the computer or there is a power cut. If you do not save your work it cannot be recalled and so you would have to key it in all over again.

METHOD

1   From the **File** menu, select: **Save As** (Figure 2.7).

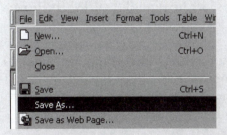

Figure 2.7   Saving a file for the first time using Save As

2   The Save As dialogue box is displayed (Figure 2.8).

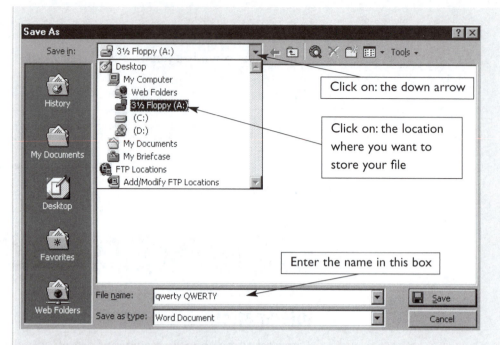

Figure 2.8 The Save As dialogue box

3   Click on: the down arrow as shown in Figure 2.8 and click on the location where you want to save your document.

Information

There are many locations where you could save your document. You may want to save it to a floppy disk. In this case select: **A:** and remember to have your disk inserted in the drive as follows:

With the front of the disk facing up (the front is the side where the label goes, without the metal circle in the centre), push the disk into the drive (metal slider first) until it clicks. The drive's **Eject** button pops out ready to use for removing the disk.

If you are saving to the computer's internal hard disk, you could save in **My Documents**. This is the default storage location. (In Chapter 5 you will learn how to manage your stored documents.)

4   In the **File name** box, double-click on the filename that is already there (e.g. **qwerty QWERTY**), and delete it by pressing: **Delete**.
5   Key in the filename **Keyboard** (case does not matter).
6   Click on: **Save**.

Information

Notice that the default filename has been replaced with the new filename (**Keyboard**) on the Title bar.

6.10 Printing

Note: You may need to refer to your printer manual for this exercise. It is assumed that your printer has already been set up to work with your computer.

Print the file **Keyboard**.

METHOD

1   Locate the printer that is connected to your computer.
2   Load it with paper.
3   Ensure it is switched on.
4   From the **File** menu, select: **Print** (Figure 2.9).

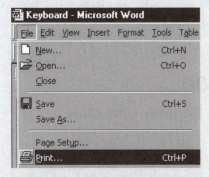

Figure 2.9   *File menu, Print*

5   The Print dialogue box is displayed (Figure 2.10):

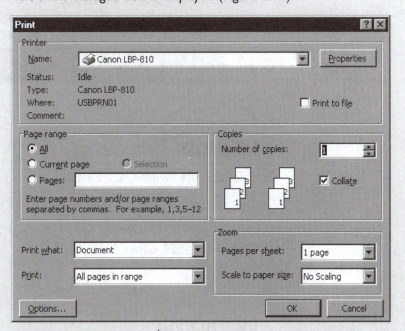

Figure 2.10   *Print dialogue box*

6   There are several default options concerning printing, such as number of copies and page range (shown in the Print dialogue box). At this stage, you should not need to change any settings, so just click on: **OK**.

Information

Quick method to print
On the toolbar, click on: the 🖨 **Print** button.

Use this if you know that you do not need to alter anything in the Print dialogue box.

6.11 Closing a file

Information

When you have finished working on a document and have saved it, it is a good idea to close it so that it is removed from your screen and is out of the way.

METHOD

From the **File** menu, select: **Close**

or

Click on: the ☒ **Close** button at the far right of the **Menu bar**.

Note: There are two **Close** buttons: the inner one is for closing the document, the other at the far top-right corner is for closing Word.

6.12 Exiting Word

METHOD

From the **File** menu, select: **Exit**

or

Click on: the ☒ **Close** button.

Information

If you forget to save the document in Word, you will be prompted to do so.

Task 6 Check

Practice 3

1 Load Word.
2 Key in the following and key in your name at the end where shown:

The Gulf Stream is a warm ocean current. It flows across the Atlantic Ocean from the Gulf of Mexico. The winters in Britain would be much longer and colder without the Gulf Stream.

[Your name]

3 Save the document with the filename **ocean**.
4 Print one copy.
5 Close the document.
6 Exit Word.

Practice 4

1 Load Word.
2 Key in the following and key in your name at the end where shown:

Distances

There are 430 miles between Birmingham and Aberdeen. It is 164 miles from Hull to Shrewsbury. It is 209 miles from York to London. All of these distances are by road. Do you know how many miles it is from Bristol to London?

[Your name]

3 Save the document with the filename **distances**.
4 Print one copy.
5 Close the document.
6 Exit Word.

Task 7 Editing

This task demonstrates some of the many advantages of using a word processor. You will discover how to make your documents error free and perfectly presented without the need to redo everything.

When you have completed this task you will have learnt how to:
- open a saved file
- move around the document
- insert text
- delete text
- resave a previously saved file
- spellcheck
- use Print Preview
- select text.

Opening a saved file

Reload the file **Keyboard** saved in Task 6.

METHOD

1   Load Word.
2   Click on the: 📂 **Open** button.
3   The Open dialogue box is displayed (Figure 2.11).
4   (If you have saved your file on a floppy disk, remember to have it inserted in the disk drive.) In the **Look in** box, click on: the down arrow and then on the location of your file.
5   Click on: the filename.
6   Click on: **Open**.

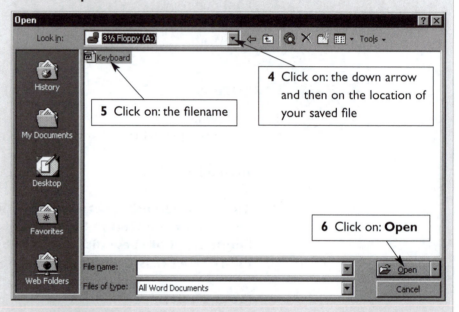

Figure 2.11   Opening a file

Moving around a document

METHOD

Here you will learn three methods to move around the document. Note: These only work when text is present, not on a blank screen.

1   Using the arrow keys.
2   Using the mouse.
3   Using two keys together: **Ctrl + Home** and **Ctrl + End**.

a   *Moving around your document using the arrow keys*
The arrow keys ← ↑ → ↓ located near the bottom right of the main keyboard) allow you to move the cursor (a flashing black vertical line) in the direction of the arrows. You can move one space forwards or backwards at a time, or you can move up or down one line at a time. If

you keep an arrow key pressed down, the cursor will move quickly through the document. Remember to release the arrow key when you reach the required place.

b   *Moving around your document using the mouse*
As you move the mouse around the screen, you will notice that it turns into an I-beam and moves with you. Move it until you have reached the required position, click: the left mouse button once and the cursor will appear where you clicked.

c   *Using **Ctrl** + **Home** and **Ctrl** + **End***
Hold down: the **Ctrl** key at the same time as the **Home** key to move to the start of your document.
Hold down: the **Ctrl** key at the same time as the **End** key to move to the end of your document.

7.3   Inserting text

Insert the word **cub** between **fox** and **jumps**.

METHOD

1   Use the mouse to position the cursor at the point where you want to insert text (in this case after the space after the word **fox**), and then key in **cub** and a space (Figure 2.12).
2   Notice how the text to the right of the cursor moves to make room for the new text.

Note: If the inserted text overwrites existing text, press: the **Insert** key (it has a 'toggle' action).

qwerty QWERTY
The quick brown fox cub |jumps over the lazy dog.

[Your name]

2 ! 4 = 1 / & 3 − 8 # 6 @ 7 : 5 ? £ % * + , 9

Figure 2.12   Inserting text

7.4   Deleting text

Delete the word **quick**. Four methods are shown below. Try each one, inserting the word **quick** after each deletion.

METHOD 1

Position the cursor to the left of the first character that you want to delete (i.e. the **q** of **quick**) and press: **Delete** until all the letters of **quick** (and the space) have been deleted.

METHOD 2

Position the cursor to the right of the last character you want to delete and press: ← **Del** (Backspace) key (top right of main keyboard) until all the letters of **quick** (and the space) have been deleted.

METHOD 3

Double-click on the word **quick** and press: **Delete**.

METHOD 4

1 Position the cursor to the left of the first character that you want to delete.
2 Hold down the left mouse button and drag the mouse over the letters in the word **quick** so that the letters in the word are selected (i.e. they are highlighted).
3 Release the mouse.
4 Press: **Delete**.

Note: This method of selecting can be used for longer portions of text.

7.5 Resaving

Save the document using the original filename **Keyboard** by clicking on the 🖫 **Save** button. Print the file. Close the file.

Information

The great thing about using a computer is that you can save your work so that you can recall it at a later date to make alterations, update it and so on. Note that the document, when saved, is referred to as a file.

Since you have already saved the first draft of this document, you will now be able to do a quick save instead of using **Save As**. This will overwrite your original with the changes you have made, but still keep the same filename, **Keyboard**. If you wanted to keep the original document intact you would need to save the document with a different name (e.g. **Keyboard2** using **Save As**). You would then have two files, the original and the amended one.

7.6　Creating a new document

Create the following new document and save with the filename **keys** and print:

I am learning about the keys on the computer keyboard. The keyboard has a standard layout. There are lots of extra keys and I am learning what they do. I am trying to be very accurate.

[Your name]

METHOD

1　With Word loaded, from the File menu, select: New (Figure 2.13).

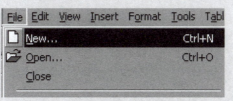

Figure 2.13　Creating a new document

2　The New box is displayed.
3　Click on: the **General** tab, then on: **Blank Document**, then on: **OK**.
4　Create and save the document in the normal way.

7.7　Spellchecking

Run the spellchecker through the document you have just created.

Information

It is always important to use the spellchecker before you print a document as it will pick up most misspelt words and provide you with a chance to correct them. Word provides an option to check spelling and grammar together, or check spelling and grammar as you type (producing red or green wavy lines under suspect text). At this stage it is more straightforward to check spelling only and I have set this option in the examples (see the Appendix for changing the default).

Note: There are limitations to the spellchecker's abilities and it may not pick up the wrong use of words (e.g. where and were, stair and stare). Although these words are spelt correctly it may be that they are being used in the wrong context.

METHOD

1   Position the cursor at the start of the document by pressing: **Ctrl +
      Home**.
2   Click on: the 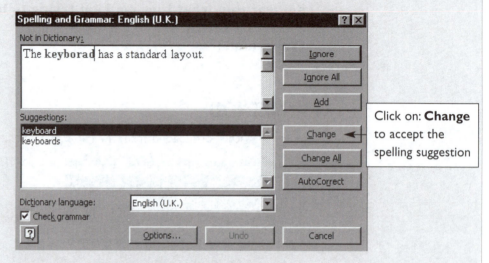 **Spelling and Grammar** button.
3   The Spelling and Grammar dialogue box is displayed (Figure 2.14).

Figure 2.14   Spelling and Grammar Dialogue box

The spellchecker will go through your text rapidly and match it with the words in its dictionary. It will highlight unrecognisable words and offer suggestions. (You may not have made any spelling errors!) In the example above, it has highlighted the word **keyborad** and it is offering its preferred replacement, **keyboard**, also highlighted in the lower box. In this case accept the suggestion by clicking on: **Change**.

If you do not want to accept a suggestion the spellchecker has made, click on: **Ignore**.

If you want to accept one of the other suggestions, click it to select it and then click on: **Change**.

The spellchecker will repeat this process until it has finished checking all the text. It will then display a message telling you that the spellcheck is complete.

Note: The spellchecker may not recognise your name or other words that would not normally be in a dictionary. When it selects such words, you should click on: **Ignore**.

Save the document when the spellcheck is finished.

7.8   Print Preview

Use Print Preview to see how your document will look and then print one copy.

METHOD

When you want to see how your document is going to look on paper before printing it, you can use Word's **Print Preview** facility.

1   Click on: the 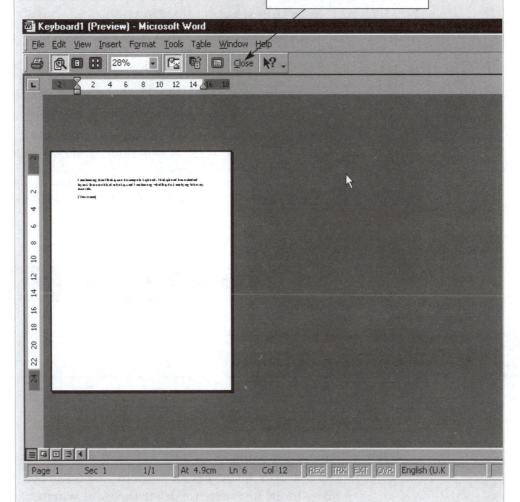 **Print Preview** button. The **Print Preview** screen appears (Figure 2.15).

Click on: **Close** to return to the document window

Figure 2.15 The Print Preview screen

Information

The cursor appears in the shape of a magnifying glass. You can zoom in to any part of the document by clicking over it with the left mouse button. To zoom out, click again.

2   Press: **Esc** or click on: **Close** to return to the document window.
3   Print in the normal way.

7.10 Selecting text

Practise different ways of selecting longer portions of text as follows:

Selecting what	Action
Whole document	**Ctrl** + **A** (held down at the same time)
One word	Double-click on: word or drag the mouse over it
One paragraph	Double-click in: selection border (i.e. to the left of the text or drag the mouse over it)
Any block of text	Click cursor at start of text, press: **Shift**. Click cursor at end of text and click. Alternatively, drag the mouse over it.
Deselect text	Click in any white space

7.11 Close the file and exit Word

Task 7 Check

Practice 5

1 Load Word.
2 Reload the file **ocean** saved in Task 6 Practice 3.
3 In the first sentence delete the word **warm**.
4 In the final sentence, insert the word **much** before the word **colder**.
5 Correct any errors you have made and spellcheck the document.
6 Resave the file with its original name.
7 Print preview and print one copy.
8 Close the file.

Practice 6

1 Reload the file **distances** saved in Task 6 Practice 4.
2 After the first sentence, insert the following sentence so that it becomes the second sentence:

There are 167 miles between Bristol and Manchester.

3 In the final sentence delete the word **London** and replace with the word **Penzance**.
4 Correct any errors you have made and spellcheck the document.

5 Resave the file with the original filename.
6 Print preview and print one copy.
7 Close the file.
8 Exit Word.

Task 8 Creating a dinner menu

For this task you will create a dinner menu. In the process you will learn how to format it to make it look decorative and add a picture and a border. You will be able to use the skills you learn here to create other attractive items such as advertisements, posters, invitations and so on. Word manages to do a very good job producing such things. However, if you get into designing in a big way, then you may prefer to use a *desktop publishing* (DTP) application, such as Microsoft Publisher.

When you have completed this task you will have learnt how to:
- switch views
- change font, size, emphasis
- align text
- change line spacing
- use WordArt
- insert a Clip Art picture
- add a border.

8.1 Switching views and keying in

METHOD

1 Load Word.

2 Switch to **Print Layout View** by clicking on: the ▭ **Print Layout View** button (bottom left of document window). (You will need to be in this view since this task contains objects that are not displayed in **Normal View** – e.g. WordArt and borders.)

3 Key in the text as shown below:

Starter

Tomato Pesto Toasties
Chicken Pittas with Red Coleslaw
Chinese Garlic Mushrooms

Main Course

Tuscan Chicken
Stuffed Plaice Rolls
Cajun Style Cod

Dessert

Fruity Bread Pudding
Apple Foam with Blackberries
Mango and Ginger Clouds

Change the headings **Starter**, **Main Course** and **Dessert** to a different font and a larger font size.

Information

The term *font* refers to the design of the characters. In Word there are numerous fonts to choose from. The default font is *Times New Roman*. This is a *serif* font. Serifs are small lines that stem from the upper and lower ends of characters. Serif fonts have such lines. *Sans serif* fonts do not have these lines. Examples:

Times New Roman is a serif font
Arial is a sans serif font

The vertical height of fonts is measured in *points* (*pt*). The default point size is 12 so when asked for a font size larger than the rest of the text, 14 pt or 16 pt would be good choices. Below are some sample point sizes:

8 pt
10 pt
12 pt
18 pt
28 pt
36 pt
48 pt

METHOD

Changing font type

1   Select the heading **Starter** so that it is highlighted. (For practice, this time use a method other than double-clicking on the word. This method is used for selecting more than one word.)

To do this:

a   Position the cursor at the beginning of the text to select – in this case the **S** of **Starter**.
b   Hold down the left mouse button and drag the I-beam pointer across the heading so that it is highlighted.
c   Release the mouse.

2 Click on the down arrow in the **Font** box (where *Times New Roman* is displayed, shown in Figure 2.16) to display fonts that are available on your computer.

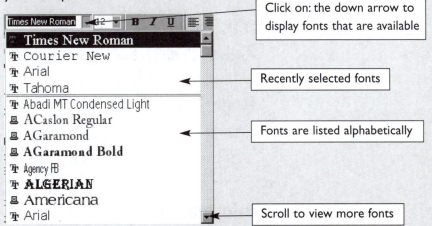

Click on: the down arrow to display fonts that are available

Recently selected fonts

Fonts are listed alphabetically

Scroll to view more fonts

Figure 2.16   Fonts available in Word

3 Click on: a font that you think will look best for your dinner menu.

Changing font size

4 With the text still selected, click on the down arrow in the **Font Size** box (Figure 2.17).

5 Click on the size required.

6 Click in a white space to deselect the text.

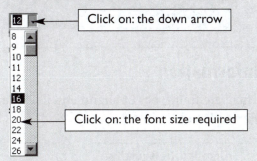

Click on: the down arrow

Click on: the font size required

Figure 2.17   Changing font size

7 Repeat these steps for each of the menu headings.

8.3   Emphasising text

Information

Emboldening, italicising or underlining text is a way of giving emphasis to the text.

Practice 7

Emboldening text.

METHOD

1   Select the text to be emboldened.
2   Click on: the **B** **Embolden** button.

Italicising text

Follow the method shown above except at step 2 click on: the *I* **Italic** button.

Underlining text

Follow the method shown above except at step 2 click on: the **U** **Underline** button.

Information

When underlining, do not extend the underline before or beyond the words to underline, as shown in the examples below:

<u>Your name</u> is correct
<u> Your name</u> is incorrect

Use the ↰ **Undo** button to undo the last actions where appropriate.

8.4   Aligning text

Information

There are four types of alignment. They can be accessed via the **Formatting** toolbar (Figure 2.18).

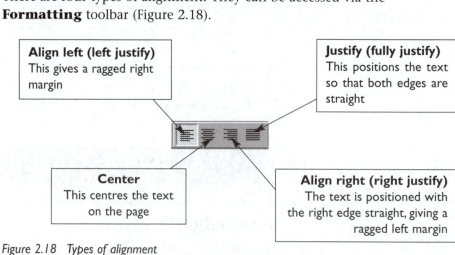

Align left (left justify)
This gives a ragged right margin

Justify (fully justify)
This positions the text so that both edges are straight

Center
This centres the text on the page

Align right (right justify)
The text is positioned with the right edge straight, giving a ragged left margin

Figure 2.18 Types of alignment

Centring text

Practice 8

Practise aligning the text. Use the **Undo** button to undo each alignment. You can also 'undo' by holding the **Ctrl** + **Z** key down at the same time.

8.5   Line spacing

Change the whole document to double line spacing.

Information

Word lets you apply a variety of line space settings (the distance between individual lines of text). Examples are *single line* spacing and *double line* spacing.

This is an example of single line spacing. The default setting is single line spacing. If the specification for a document is single line spacing, then usually you need do nothing.

This is an example of double line spacing. There is one blank line left

between lines of text. It is often used when a section needs extra emphasis.

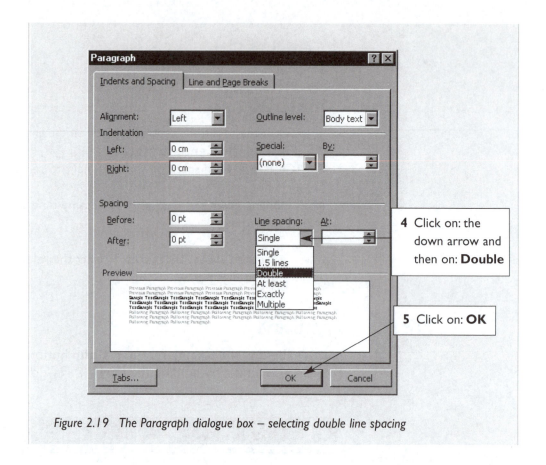

Figure 2.19   The Paragraph dialogue box – selecting double line spacing

The panel next to the Line spacing dropdown reads:

> **4** Click on: the down arrow and then on: **Double**

> **5** Click on: **OK**

8.6   Inserting WordArt

Insert the heading for your dinner menu **Celebration Dinner** using WordArt.

Information

Using the WordArt facilities of Word you are able to insert imaginative text into your documents. WordArt can be used to create things like logos. *Note*: It is not manipulated in the same way as the text we have looked at in the previous sections.

METHOD

1   Position the cursor where you want the heading to be. Press: **Ctrl + Home** to go to the top of the document. Create line spaces if you need to by pressing: **Enter**. Then click the mouse at the top of the document.

2   From the **Insert** menu, select: **Picture**, then **WordArt** (Figure 2.20).

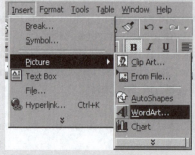

Figure 2.20   Inserting WordArt

3   The WordArt Gallery is displayed (Figure 2.21).

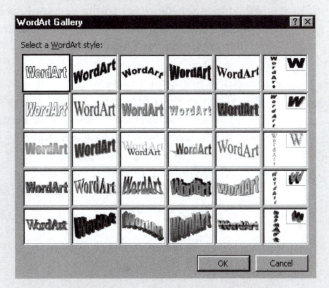

Figure 2.21   WordArt Gallery

4   Click on: a WordArt style box that you like, then on: **OK**.
5   The Edit WordArt Text box is displayed (Figure 2.22).

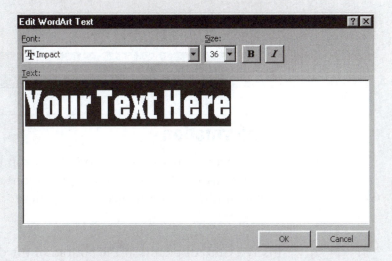

Figure 2.22   Entering WordArt text

6   In the **Text** box, key in the text **Celebration Dinner**. *Note:* You can change the font, size and embolden and italicise in this box.
7   Click on: **OK**.
8   The WordArt text is inserted in the document (Figure 2.23).

Figure 2.23   WordArt inserted and WordArt toolbar appears

9   Click on: the WordArt to select it.

10   Move the WordArt to the required position as follows:

    a Hold down the left mouse button over the selection.

    b A four-point arrow appears.

    c Drag to the required position.

    d Release the mouse.

11   The WordArt object has sizing handles around the edges so that you can make it bigger or smaller as follows:

    a Position the mouse on a handle.

    b A two-point arrow appears.

    c Hold down the left mouse button.

    d Drag the handle to the required position.

    e Release the mouse.

Note: To preserve the same aspect ratio (i.e. not make fatter or thinner), drag from a corner.

12   The WordArt also has a yellow diamond shape that can be used to distort it. It is fun to experiment and discover what you can do with WordArt using the **WordArt** toolbar. It is quite straightforward, so enjoy yourself!

8.7   Inserting a Clip Art picture

Information

Clip Art is ready-drawn artwork. Microsoft Office has a Clip Gallery (that can be used with other Office applications as well as Word). This gallery contains Clip Art arranged in categories for you to choose from.

Insert a Clip Art picture at the bottom of the dinner menu.

METHOD

1   Position the cursor where you want the picture to be.

2   From the **Insert** menu, select: **Picture**, then: **ClipArt**.

3   The **Insert ClipArt** box is displayed (Figure 2.24).

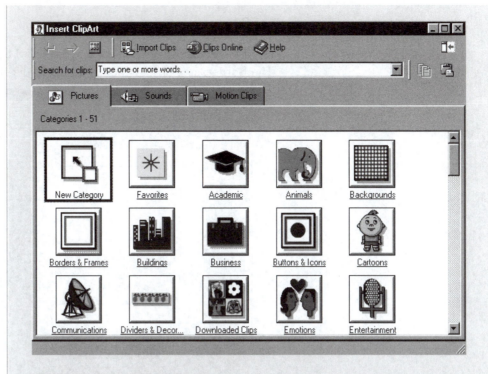

Figure 2.24 Inserting a picture

4 Click on a category and then on a suitable clip.
5 Click on: the **Insert Clip** button (Figure 2.25).

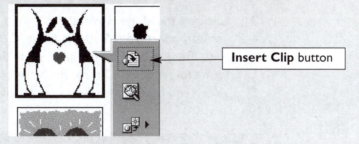

Insert Clip button

Figure 2.25 Insert Clip button

6 The picture is inserted into the document.
7 Close the Insert ClipArt box.
8 Resize and reposition it following the WordArt methods so that it fits on one page.

Information

There are lots of pictures to choose from. Use the ⬅ **Back** button to return to the categories.

8.8 Adding a border

Add a page border around your dinner menu.

METHOD

1   From the **Format** menu, select: **Borders and Shading**.
2   The Borders and Shading box is displayed (Figure 2.26).

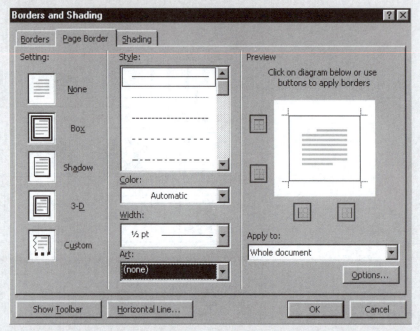

Figure 2.26   Borders and Shading box

3   Click on: the **Page Border** tab.
4   You can select from **Setting**, **Style**, **Colour**, **Width** and **Art** boxes.
    Note: The Art box choices are fun for things such as menus and posters (don't forget to scroll through the selections).
5   When you have made the selections, click on: **OK**.

8.9 Save and print the document

Save your document with the name **Menu**. Print Preview to check that it looks OK. When you are satisfied with it, print one copy.

It will look similar to Figure 2.27.

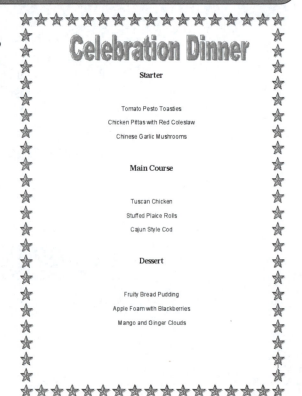

Figure 2.27   Finished menu

Task 8 Check

Practice 9

1 Create a poster with the following information:

GRAND AUCTION

Saturday 16 November

Town Hall

Starting at 2 o'clock

Viewings in the morning

Entry £1.00

Refreshments available

All proceeds to go to local charities

2 Add a picture, a page border and some WordArt.
3 Save the document with a suitable filename. (Choose a descriptive filename so that you will be able to locate it easily at a later date.)
4 Print one copy.

Practice 10

1 Create an advertisement with the following information:

FOR SALE

3 SEATER SOFA

Navy blue leather

Very good condition

To view please telephone Brian on 723491

Buyer collects

2 Format the advertisement for an eye-catching effect.
3 Insert a picture and a border.
4 Save the document with a suitable filename.
5 Print one copy.

Task 9 | Creating an agenda and minutes

This task will be helpful if you need to produce agendas and minutes in a formal/semi-formal setting (e.g. school/playgroup association, church committee or local council). It shows possible layouts you could use. *Note*: Some organisations may insist you adhere to their own in-house style.

When you have completed this task you will have learnt how to:
● lay out an agenda and minutes
● create numbered/bulleted lists.

9.1 Creating an agenda

METHOD

1   Load Word.
2   With a new document displayed, set the document to double line spacing using the **Format** menu.
3   Key in text up to the start of the numbered list:

THE HEMSLEY COMPANY

Directors' Meeting to be held on

10 February 2003 at 10.00 am in the Board Room

AGENDA
1   **Apologies for absence**
2   **Election of Chairperson**
3   **Reading of notice of meeting by secretary**
4   **Reading by secretary of minutes of last meeting**
5   **Matters arising from the minutes as read**
6   **Reading by secretary of any correspondence received**
7   **Opening comments from the Chair**
8   **Any business adjourned from last meeting**
9   **Financial matters**
10 **Reports by sub-committees, working parties**
11 **Motions to be placed before the meeting**
12 **Date of next meeting**
13 **Any other minor matters arising**

9.2 Creating a numbered list

METHOD

1 Click on: the ⠿☰ **Numbering** button.
2 The number 1 appears at the start of the line.
3 Key in the text for item 1 and press: **Enter**.
4 The number 2 appears automatically at the start of the next line.
5 Continue until the list is complete.

Information

Working with bulleted/numbered lists

Bulleted lists have a symbol (e.g. a dot, square or arrow) and can be created in the same way as numbered lists but using the ☰ **Bullets** button. Bulleted lists can be used when the items in the list do not need to be in a particular order. Bullets and numbers can take many forms. To change them:

1 Select the list.
2 From the **Format** menu, select: **Bullets and Numbering**.
3 The Bullets and Numbering box is displayed (Figure 2.28).
4 Click on the preferred type.
5 Click on: **OK**.

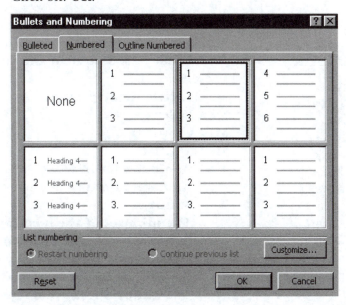

Figure 2.28 Selecting number/bullet type

To remove numbers/bullets
1 Select the numbered/bulleted list.
2 Click on: the **Numbering/Bullets** button as appropriate.

Repositioning the cursor at the margin

When working with bullets/numbering, sometimes the cursor does not position itself at the margin. If you want to move the cursor back to the margin use the ⠿≣ **Decrease Indent** toolbar button.

9.3 Save and print the document

Spellcheck, save (using a suitable filename) and print the document.

9.4 Creating minutes

METHOD

1   Load Word.
2   Create the following minutes document.

   Note: This document has lines of text in between the numbered lines. To delete unwanted automatic numbers, click on: the **Numbering** button. If necessary, use the ⯐ **Increase Indent** and ⯐ **Decrease Indent** buttons to position the start of new lines. After keying in the text lines, start the next number by clicking on: the **Numbering** button.

3   Spellcheck, save and print one copy.

THE HEMSLEY COMPANY
Minutes of the Directors' meeting held on
10 February 2003 at 10.00 am in the Board Room
Present:
Mrs B Little (Chairperson)
Miss V Neck
Mrs A N Other
Mr C D ROM
1   **Apologies for absence**
     Apologies for absence were received from Mr B Gone.
2   **Minutes**
     The minutes of the meeting of 10 January 2003 were taken as read. The following amendment was made: Minute No 4 the monetary amount of £300 was incorrect and was changed to £200.
     The minutes were then approved as a correct record and signed by the Chairperson.
3   **Matters arising**
     Minute No 6
     [Insert details of this matter here and any action needed.]
4   **Correspondence**
     [Insert details of correspondence here and any action needed.]
5   **Date of next meeting**
     It was agreed that the next meeting will be held on 10 March 2003 at 11.00 am in the Board Room.
6   **There being no further business, the Chairperson declared the meeting closed at 11:55 am.**

Useful Info

HARD SPACES

It is better not to split some words at line ends e.g. Mr Brown – Mr and Brown should be on the same line. A hard space keeps the words on either side of it together. To insert a hard space:
Instead of just pressing the spacebar between the words, press:
CTRL + SHIFT + Spacebar

Task 9 — Check

✓ Are you familiar with the following?

Layout of an agenda	
Layout of minutes	
Creating numbered/bulleted lists	

Task 10 — Creating a letter and printing an envelope

For this task you will create a letter and envelope. A sample letter (see page 52) for you to key in shows a typical business letter layout. You have already learnt most of the skills required to produce a letter like this one. However, this task also introduces you to **Page Setup**. If you use this facility you can make sure your letter will look well spaced on the page. Printing an envelope is also covered.

When you have completed this task you will have learnt how to:
- lay out a letter
- use Page Setup
- create an envelope.

10.1 Creating a letter

METHOD

1 Load Word.
2 Examine the letter layout on page 52 and then key it in.
3 Spellcheck and save the document.
4 Print one copy.

Example letter layout

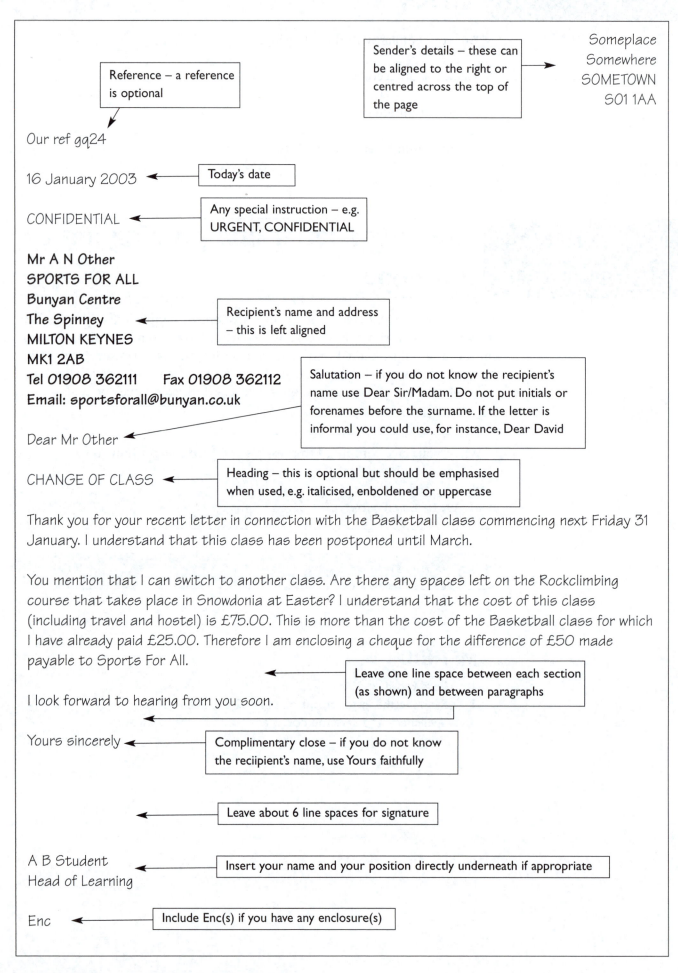

Reference – a reference is optional

Sender's details – these can be aligned to the right or centred across the top of the page

Someplace
Somewhere
SOMETOWN
S01 1AA

Our ref gq24

16 January 2003 ← Today's date

CONFIDENTIAL ← Any special instruction – e.g. URGENT, CONFIDENTIAL

Mr A N Other
SPORTS FOR ALL
Bunyan Centre
The Spinney ← Recipient's name and address – this is left aligned
MILTON KEYNES
MK1 2AB
Tel 01908 362111   Fax 01908 362112
Email: sportsforall@bunyan.co.uk

Dear Mr Other ← Salutation – if you do not know the recipient's name use Dear Sir/Madam. Do not put initials or forenames before the surname. If the letter is informal you could use, for instance, Dear David

CHANGE OF CLASS ← Heading – this is optional but should be emphasised when used, e.g. italicised, enboldened or uppercase

Thank you for your recent letter in connection with the Basketball class commencing next Friday 31 January. I understand that this class has been postponed until March.

You mention that I can switch to another class. Are there any spaces left on the Rockclimbing course that takes place in Snowdonia at Easter? I understand that the cost of this class (including travel and hostel) is £75.00. This is more than the cost of the Basketball class for which I have already paid £25.00. Therefore I am enclosing a cheque for the difference of £50 made payable to Sports For All.

← Leave one line space between each section (as shown) and between paragraphs

I look forward to hearing from you soon.

Yours sincerely ← Complimentary close – if you do not know the reciipient's name, use Yours faithfully

← Leave about 6 line spaces for signature

A B Student ← Insert your name and your position directly underneath if appropriate
Head of Learning

Enc ← Include Enc(s) if you have any enclosure(s)

10.2 Page setup

In some instances you may find that your letter is a bit cramped or that it doesn't quite fit on one page. To remedy such situations, you can use **Page Setup** to alter margins. Margins are the blank space at the top, bottom and sides of text that will be printed on your document (Figure 2.29). Page Setup can be used at any time whilst working on the document.

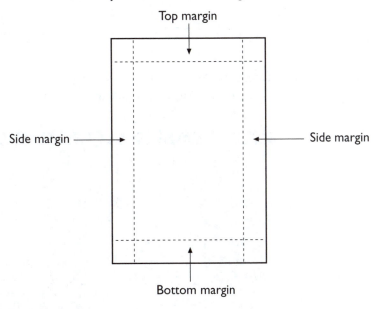

Figure 2.29   Page layout

METHOD

Note: Before following these instructions, have a look at the horizontal ruler (Figure 2.30). This shows the default width that text entered on the page will be (line length). Make a note of this measurement so that you can see the difference after resetting the margins.

Figure 2.30   Horizontal ruler

Line length end

1   From the **File** menu, select: **Page Setup** (Figure 2.31).

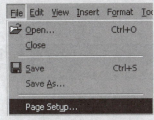

Figure 2.31   Selecting Page Setup

2   The Page Setup dialogue box is displayed (Figure 2.32).
3   Click on: the **Paper Size** tab and, in the **Paper Size** box, select: **A4** (A4 is the standard paper size in the UK).

Note: You can select **Orientation** (i.e. **Portrait** or **Landscape**). Portrait has the narrow edge at the top and landscape has the wide edge at the top. Use **Portrait** for letters.

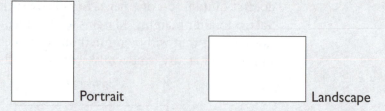

Portrait   Landscape

4   Click on: **OK**.

5   Select the **Margins** tab. This shows the default margins set by Word – i.e. **Left** and **Right** margins are 3.17 cm, **Top** and **Bottom** margins are 2.54 cm (Figure 2.32).

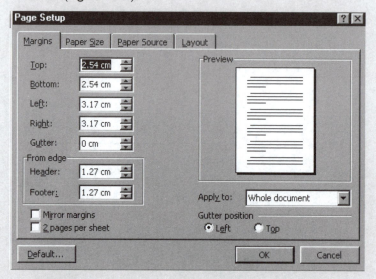

Figure 2.32   Setting margins

6   To make the margins narrower, click in the **Left** box and delete 3.17 cm and key in a new measurement (e.g. 2 cm).

7   Do the same in the **Right** box.

8   Click on: **OK**.

9   You are returned to the document window.

10 Check the horizontal ruler to see the change. The left and right margins are now narrower so the line length is longer. This means that you should be able to fit more text on the page.

10.3   Printing an envelope

METHOD

1   With the letter document on screen, select the recipient's address.

2   From the **Tools** menu, select: **Envelopes and Labels**.

3   The Envelopes and Labels box is displayed (Figure 2.33).

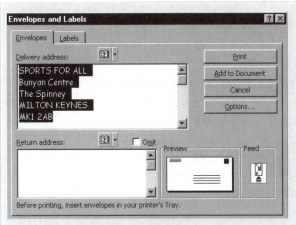

Figure 2.33   Envelopes and Labels box

4 Click on: **Options**.
5 The Envelope Options box is displayed (Figure 2.34).

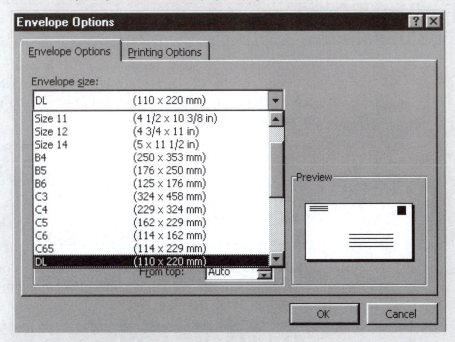

Figure 2.34   Envelope Options

6   Measure your envelope and select the envelope size (**DL** is a standard
    business envelope size).
7   Click on: **OK**.
8   You are returned to the Envelopes and Labels box.
9   Ensure that you have an envelope loaded in your printer (you may need
    to check your printer user guide). There is guide to the correct way to
    load the envelope into the printer in the **Feed** section of the
    Envelopes and Labels box.
10 Click on: **Print**.

Task 10 | Check

Are you familiar with the following?

Layout of a letter	
Changing margins	
Changing page orientation	
Printing an envelope	

Task 11 | Creating a curriculum vitae

A curriculum vitae (CV) can be presented in many different ways. This task sets out one possible CV layout indicating details of what should be included. Of course, you may want to set out your own CV differently to draw attention to your most appropriate assets.

When you have completed this task you will have learnt how to:
- produce a sample CV layout and what to include on the CV
- line up text
- use tables.

Curriculum vitae comes from the Latin meaning 'the way your life has run', sometimes known as a résumé, from the French meaning 'summary'.

11.1 Layout of CV

The CV on page 57 shows a typical layout and gives advice on what to include. Study this carefully and decide if it will work for you. Based on the layout given, produce a CV entering details (your own or made up). You may want to use tabs or Word's Table facility in some sections. You can practise both to see which you prefer.

11.2 Simple tabulation

When laying out a document such as a CV, you may find it useful to know about tabs. Tabs enable you to line up text precisely. You should never rely on the space bar for exact alignment. The alignment may look OK on screen but when printed it does not produce accurate alignment results. Working with tabs can be quite advanced but we will use only basic methods in this book.

Example CV

CURRICULUM VITAE

Gregory Bright
17 Forest Gardens
Bristol
BS8 2DJ

Personal Details

Home Telephone:
Work Telephone:
Mobile:
Email:
Date of Birth:
Marital Status (Optional):
Driving Licence:
Nationality:

Qualifications

Starting with your highest achievement, list all exams completed, i.e. Degrees, A levels, GNVQs, NVQs, AS levels, GCSEs and so on. Give dates, place of study and grades (grades are optional).

Qualification	Place of Study	Date	Grade (optional)

Skills

- List all the skills you have, i.e. computer packages, language skills, keyboard skills
- Short course achievements
- Give special emphasis to those relevant to the job

Employment History

Starting with your current or most recent job, give the following information:

Position and employer	Start date	End date	Your responsibilities	Salary	Reason for leaving

It is never wise to criticise previous employers so don't be tempted!
Do not leave any gaps. If there are gaps give reasons for these and put a positive slant.

Interests

List your main interests. Concentrate on those that may be relevant to the job.

References

Two referees are usually sufficient, for example your previous two employers. It is polite to approach these referees first so that they know a reference request may be on its way.

Examining tabs

METHOD

1   Load Word and a new document.
2   By default tabs are set every 1.27 cm from the left margin.
3   Press: the **Tab** key to move from one tab stop to the next.
4   You can also use the toolbar buttons ▤ ▤ **Decrease Indent/ Increase Indent** to move between tab stops.

Using tabs you can set up columns of text. Tabs could be used in the Qualifications and Employment History sections of the CV. However, you may find that an easier method is to use a table.

11.3   Inserting a table

Tables are relatively easy to produce and work with. They are very useful for all sorts of documents, including CVs. Because of their versatility, they are covered here in some detail.

Open a new Word document and create the following table using the Table facility:

Qualification	Place of Study	Date	Grade
A level English	Results College, London	June 2001	D
OCR CLAIT	Results College, London	December 2001	Pass
GCSE	Russell School, Leeds	June 1999	
French			A
English			B
History			D

METHOD

1   Position the cursor where you want the top left corner of the table to be.
2   Press the left mouse button and hold it down over the ▦ **Insert Table** button: a grid appears.
3   Drag the mouse across and down the grid to result in the number of columns and rows required for the table (4 columns and 7 rows, including a blank row after the headings; Figure 2.35). Release the mouse.

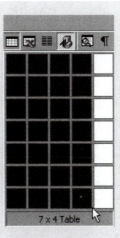

Figure 2.35   Setting cells for a new table

4   The empty table appears in your document.

5   Key in the table's text, pressing **Tab** to move to the next entry position (or use the arrow keys).

Information

If you press **Enter** by mistake, a line space will appear. Press: ← **Del** (Backspace) key to remove the line space.

Working with borders

By default the table will automatically have borders around the table's cells. Use the following method to remove the borders on the table.

METHOD

I   Position the cursor anywhere in the table and, from the **Table** menu, select: **Select**, then: **Table**.

2   From the toolbar, click on the down arrow next to the **Border** button. Click on: **No Border** as shown in Figure 2.36.

Click on: this down arrow

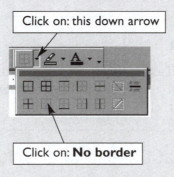

Click on: **No border**

Figure 2.36   Deleting borders

Note: There are other border options available. Experiment with adding/removing borders. Right-clicking over the table will bring up the pop-up menu shown in Figure 2.37.

Figure 2.37 The pop-up table menu

3 Select: **Borders and Shading** to access the Borders and Shading dialogue box (Figure 2.38) where, with the **Borders** tab selected, further preferences can be set (e.g. line widths, colours and styles).

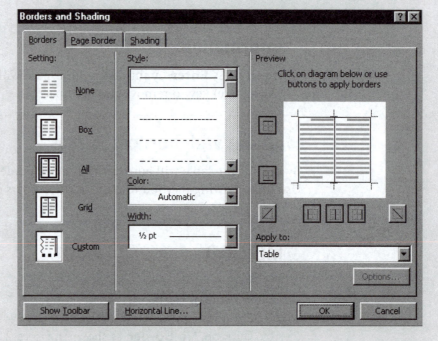

Figure 2.38 Select border preferences from here

Information

In addition to selecting the entire table, individual cells or groups of cells can be selected so that they can have different borders from the rest of the table. To deselect, click in a white space.

Adding rows at the end of a table

Add a row at the bottom of the table and key in the following in the relevant places:

Geography			D

1   Position the cursor after the last table entry (i.e. the B grade for English).
2   Press: **Tab**. A new row is created.
3   Key in the text.

Inserting rows within the table

Insert a row between the one displaying **A Level English** and **OCR CLAIT** and insert the text:

OCR IBT II	Results College, London	June 2001	Pass

1   Select the row below where you want to insert the new row, by dragging the mouse over it.
2   From the **Table** menu, select: **Insert**, then: **Rows Above** (Figure 2.39).

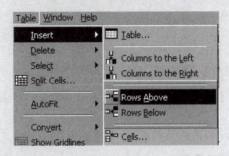

Figure 2.39   Inserting rows

3   Key in the text.

Deleting rows

Delete the row containing **French**.

1   Select the row to be deleted.
2   Right-click over the selection; a pop-up menu appears (Figure 2.40).
3   Select: **Delete Cells**. The Delete Cells box appears (Figure 2.41). Click next to **Delete entire row**. Click on: **OK**.

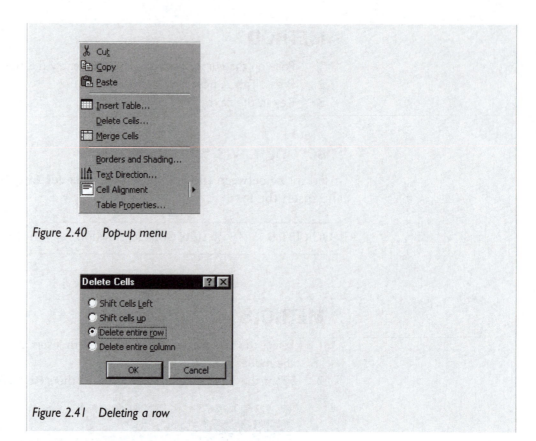

Figure 2.40   Pop-up menu

Figure 2.41   Deleting a row

Deleting columns

Use the following method if you want to delete columns.

METHOD

1   Select the column to delete by hovering over the line at the top of the column. When a thick black arrow appears, click the mouse.
2   Right-click over the selection.
3   From the pop-up menu, select: **Delete Columns** (Figure 2.42).

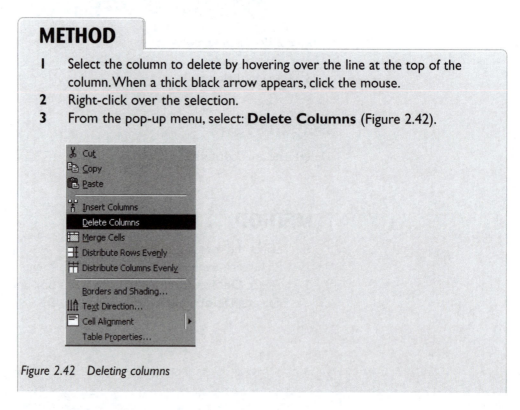

Figure 2.42   Deleting columns

Inserting columns

Use the following method if you want to insert columns.

METHOD

1 Select the column to the right of the required position for the new column.
2 Right-click over the selection.
3 From the pop-up menu, select: **Insert Columns**.
4 Key in the text.

Information

Deleting an entire table
Select the table by clicking anywhere within it and, from the **Table** menu, select: **Delete**, **Table**. Click on: the **Undo** button to reinstate the table!

Changing cell attributes

You can format as follows.

METHOD

1 Select the cells to format.
2 Format in the usual way with the toolbar buttons (e.g. bold, italic, centre, change font and size and so on).

Change the background of the heading cells to a colour other than white

METHOD

1 Select the cells and right-click to bring up a pop-up menu.
2 Select: **Borders and Shading**.
3 Ensure the **Shading** tab is selected.
4 Click on: a colour. Click on: **OK**.
5 Click outside the table to show colour in the cell.

Changing column width

METHOD

1 Select the column to change.
2 Drag the column border to the required width position.

Information

Tables are created with standard cell widths and heights. Change them by selecting them and dragging the borders (as above) or you can use **AutoFit** as follows:

With the table or cell(s) selected, from the **Table** menu, select: **AutoFit**, **AutoFit to Contents**.

Using automatic table formatting

Information

Word has several table formats to select from.

To Autoformat a table:
1   Position the cursor in the table.
2   From the **Table** menu, select: **Table AutoFormat**.
3   Select from the **Formats** list.

Experiment with the formats. Notice that some will not suit the table since they have headings in the first column.

Task 11   Check

✓ Are you familiar with the following?

Layout for a CV	
Contents of a CV	
Lining up text	
Inserting a table	
Working with tables	

Quick Reference Guide: Word

Action	Keyboard	Mouse	Right-mouse menu	Menu
Align left	**Ctrl + L**	Click: the **Align Left** button	**Paragraph**	**Format, Paragraph**
			Select **Left** from the **Alignment:** drop-down menu	
Bold text	Select text to embolden			
	Ctrl + B	Click: the **B Bold** button	**Font**	**Format, Font**
			Select: **Bold** from the **Font style:** menu	
Borders, whole page	**Format, Borders and Shading** Select the border options you require			
Capitals (blocked)	**Caps Lock** Key in the text **Caps Lock** again to remove			Select text to be changed to capitals: **Format, Change Case, UPPERCASE**
Centre text	Select the text			
	Ctrl + E	Click: the **Center** button	**Paragraph**	**Format, Paragraph**
			Select: **Centered** from the **Alignment:** drop-down menu	
Change case	Select the text to be changed From the **Format** menu, select: **Change Case** Select the appropriate case			
Close a file	**Ctrl + W**	Click: the **Close** button		**File, Close**
Delete a character	Press: **Delete** to delete the character to the right of the cursor Press: ← (Backspace) to delete the character to the left of the cursor			
Delete a word	Double-click: the word to select it. Press: **Delete**			
Envelope				**Tools, Envelopes and Labels**
Exit Word		Click: the **Close** button		**File, Exit**
Font size	Select the text you want to change	Click: the down arrow next to the **Font Size** box Select: the font size you require	**Font**	**Format, Font**
			Select: the required size from the **Size:** menu	
Font	Select the text you want to change			
		Click: the down arrow next to the **Font** box Select: the font you require	**Font**	**Format, Font**
			Select: the required font from the **Font:** menu	
Help	**F1**			**Help, Microsoft Word Help**
	Shift + F1			**Help, What's This?**
Indenting		Click: the **Increase Indent** button	**Paragraph, Indents and Spacing**	**Format, Paragraph, Indents and Spacing**
to remove indent		Click: the **Decrease Indent** button	In the **Indentation** section, select your options as appropriate	

Action	Keyboard	Mouse	Right-mouse menu	Menu
Insert Clip Art				**Insert**, *either* **Picture**, **Clip Art** Resize using handles
Insert text	Position the cursor where you want the text to appear Key in the text			
Italicise	Select: text to italicise			
	Ctrl +I	Click: the *I* **Italic** button	**Font**	**Format**, **Font**
			Select: **Italic** from the **Font Style** menu	
Justify text	**Ctrl + J**	Click: the **Justify** icon	**Paragraph**	**Format**, **Paragraph**
			Select **Justified** from the **Alignment:** drop-down menu	
Line length, changing		Use the ruler (see below)		**File**, **Page Setup**, **Margins**
Line space	Press: **Enter** twice			
Line spacing			**Paragraph**	**Format**, **Paragraph**, **Indents and Spacing**
			In the **Spacing** section, select the options you require	
Lists, bulleted and numbered		Click: the **Numbering** *or* **Bullets** button	**Bullets and Numbering**	**Format**, **Bullets and Numbering**
Load Word	In Windows 98 desktop			
		Double-click: the **Word** shortcut icon		**Start**, **Programs**, **Microsoft Word**
Moving around the document	Use the cursor keys (see separate table for more)	Click in the required position		
New file, creating	**Ctrl + N**	Click: the **New** button		**File**, **New**
Open an existing file	**Ctrl + O**	Click: the **Open** button		**File**, **Open**
	Select the appropriate directory and filename Click: **Open**			
Page Setup				**File**, **Page Setup** (choose from **Margins**, **Paper Size**, **Paper Source**, **Layout**)
Paper size	(See Page Setup)			
Print file	**Ctrl + P** Select the options you need Press: **Enter**	Click: the **Print** button		**File**, **Print** Select the options you need and click **OK**
Print Preview		Click: the **Print Preview** button		**File**, **Print Preview**
Remove text emphasis	Select: text to be changed **Ctrl + B** (remove bold) **Ctrl + I** (remove italics) **Ctrl + U** (remove underline)	Click: the appropriate button: **B** *I* **U**	**Font**	**Format**, **Font** Select **Regular** from the **Font Style:** menu

Action	Keyboard	Mouse	Right-mouse menu	Menu
Save	**Ctrl + S**	Click: the 💾 **Save** button		**F**ile, **S**ave
	If you have not already saved the file you will be prompted to specify the directory and to name the file. If you have already done this, Word will automatically save it.			
Save using a different name or to a different drive or folder	Select the appropriate drive and change the filename if relevant. Click: **Save**			**F**ile, **S**ave **A**s
Select text	See separate table			
Spellcheck	**F7**	Click: the **Spelling** button		**T**ools, **S**pelling and Grammar
Tables		Click: the **Insert Table** button		**T**able, **I**nsert, **T**able
	See below			
Toolbar, modify				**V**iew, **T**oolbars, **C**ustomize
Undo	**Ctrl + Z**	Click: the **Undo** button		**E**dit, **U**ndo Typing
View	Click: the appropriate **View** button			**V**iew

Moving around the document

Move	Keyboard action
to top of document	**Ctrl + Home**
to end of document	**Ctrl + End**
left word by word	**Ctrl + ←**
right word by word	**Ctrl + →**
to end of line	**End**
to start of line	**Home**

Selecting text

Text can be selected by dragging the mouse across it. Here are some other methods:

Selecting what	Action
Whole document	**Ctrl + A**
One word	Double-click on word
One paragraph	Double-click in selection border
Any block of text	Click cursor at start of text, press: **Shift**. Click cursor at end of text and click
Deselect text	Click in any white space

Indentation using the ruler

Select the text you want to indent. Drag the respective markers (shown below) on the ruler to the location you want:

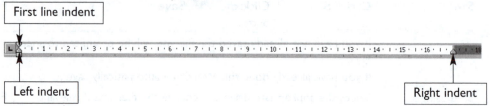

Working with tables

Inserting rows/columns
Select the row below where you want to insert new rows, or select the column to the right of where you want to insert new columns. Right-click over the selection. From the pop-up menu, select: **Insert Rows** or **Insert Columns**.

Adding a row at the end of a table
Click in: the last cell of the last row and press: **Tab**.

Adding a column to the right of the last column in a table
Click: just outside the right-hand column. From the **Table** menu, select: **Select Column**, right-click over selection, select: **Insert Columns**.

Deleting a table and its contents
Select the table by clicking anywhere in it. From the **Table** menu, select: **Select Table**. Click on: the **Cut** button.

Deleting cells, rows or columns from a table
Select the cells, rows or columns you want to delete. Right-click over the selection and select: **Delete Cells**.

Ensuring that the contents fit the cells
Select the appropriate cells.
From the **Table** menu, select: **AutoFit**, **AutoFit to Contents**

or

Select the column/row to change and drag the column/row border to the required position.

Copying formatting

1   Select text to copy.
2   Click: the **Format Painter** button.
3   Double-click on: the **Format Painter** button to copy to several pieces of text.
4   Select text to copy format to.

Chapter 3 Working with spreadsheets

This chapter has six tasks for you to try. The first three contain the basics of using a spreadsheet application. These tasks take you step by step through structured exercises so that you will have a solid introduction to how spreadsheets work. They also have optional consolidation exercises to hone newfound skills. You should then feel confident when working through some applications of spreadsheets examples in Tasks 15, 16 and 17. If you're not too keen on working with numbers, you will discover that it has never been so easy. If you love working with numbers, you will marvel at the spreadsheet's capabilities.

Task 12 First steps with spreadsheets 1

This task introduces the main principles of spreadsheets and demonstrates how to build the very simplest. By concentrating on spreadsheet facilities (instead of keying in loads of data) it encourages understanding of the processes involved. It is important to develop such understanding at this early stage in order to progress.

> When you have completed this task you will have learnt how to:
> - know when and why to use a spreadsheet
> - load Excel
> - enter spreadsheet content
> - use simple formulae
> - save the spreadsheet
> - print the spreadsheet
> - print the spreadsheet showing formulae
> - close the spreadsheet file
> - exit Excel.

12.1 What is a spreadsheet application?

A spreadsheet application (this book uses Microsoft Excel) has some aspects of a filing system and some of a calculator. It consists of a large table, or grid, in which you enter data and text for calculations to be carried out. The spreadsheet program performs calculations as instructed by you. Spreadsheets are easily edited and when changes are made new values are recalculated automatically. Spreadsheets are very fast, accurate and flexible. You can print them or parts of them and save them to disk to edit or update later. Spreadsheets are used for various tasks from accounting, household budgets, maintaining league football results to scientific analysis results and 'what if' scenarios. They can also be used for creating and maintaining lists, for example shopping lists and CD or record collections. You will learn and appreciate the advantages of spreadsheet applications as you progress through this chapter.

METHOD

Load Excel in the same way as other Office 2000 applications, this time selecting: 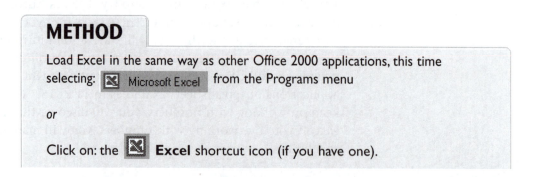 Microsoft Excel   from the Programs menu

or

Click on: the ⊠ **Excel** shortcut icon (if you have one).

12.3   **Understanding the parts of Excel**

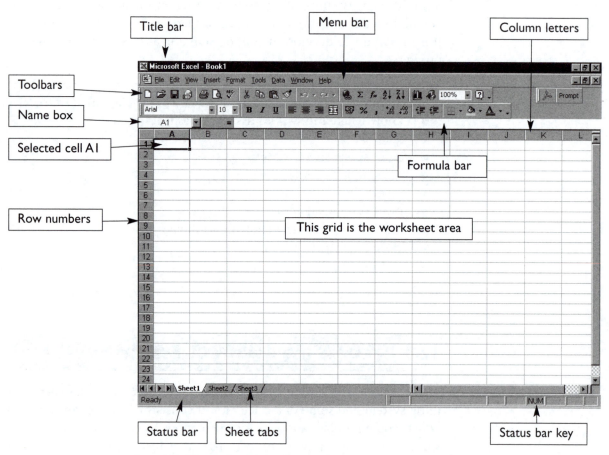

Figure 3.1   The application window

- The **Title** bar and **Menu** bar are at the top of the application window.
- The **Menu** bar has a set of *drop-down* menus that provide access to all of Excel's features.
- The **toolbar** is a row of buttons and selection boxes that, in most cases, provide shortcuts to the menu options or quick ways of entering values. (In Figure 3.1 the *Standard* and *Formatting* toolbars are shown.)
- The **Formula** bar displays the entry in a selected cell on your spreadsheet.
- The **Name** box displays the active cell reference.

- The **Sheet tabs** allow you to move from one sheet to the next. (You can have more than one spreadsheet in an Excel document. Together these sheets are known as a *Workbook*.)
- The **Status** bar, located at the bottom of the window, displays messages about current events as you work on the spreadsheet.
- The **Status bar key** shows **NUM** (by default). This denotes that the **Num Lock** key on your keyboard will enable you to use the number keys 0 to 9 (at the right of the keyboard) to enter numbers more quickly. If you want to use the movement key options instead (e.g. arrows, Home), press: the **Num Lock** key to turn Num Lock off.
- **The Worksheet Area** is the area between the Formula bar and the Status bar where your document (spreadsheet) is displayed.

It consists of cells, each with their own cell reference (e.g. A1, B7, F9).
Rows go across and are labelled 1, 2, 3, 4 ...
Columns go down and are labelled A, B, C, D ...

Figure 3.2 shows the position of cell C6.

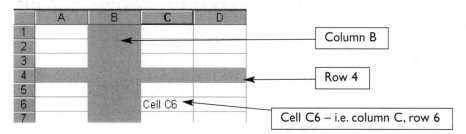

Figure 3.2   Cell references

 ## Practice 11

Moving around the spreadsheet.

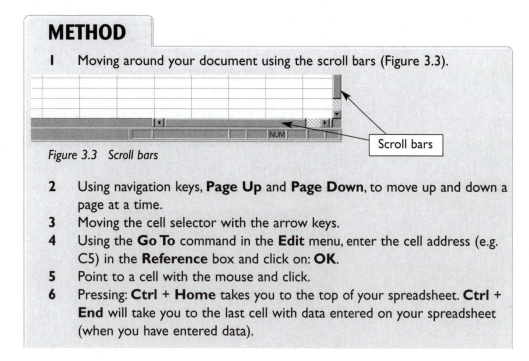

METHOD

I   Moving around your document using the scroll bars (Figure 3.3).

Figure 3.3   Scroll bars

2   Using navigation keys, **Page Up** and **Page Down**, to move up and down a page at a time.
3   Moving the cell selector with the arrow keys.
4   Using the **Go To** command in the **Edit** menu, enter the cell address (e.g. C5) in the **Reference** box and click on: **OK**.
5   Point to a cell with the mouse and click.
6   Pressing: **Ctrl + Home** takes you to the top of your spreadsheet. **Ctrl + End** will take you to the last cell with data entered on your spreadsheet (when you have entered data).

12.4 Spreadsheet contents

You can enter:

- text
- numeric data
- formulae.

Text entries are used for titles, headings and any notes. They are entries that you do not want to manipulate arithmetically.

Numeric data consists of numbers you want to add, subtract, multiply, divide and use in formulae.

Formulae are used to calculate the value of a cell from the contents of other cells. For instance, formulae may be used to calculate totals or averages. *Formulae always start with an = sign*. A typical formula could look like this:

Note: The following operators (symbols) are used in formulae:

+ ADD   - SUBTRACT * MULTIPLY / DIVIDE

=A1+A2

or

=SUM(A1:A6)

or

=B5+C9-B3

or

=D5*A7

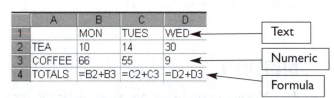

Figure 3.4 *Types of spreadsheet entry*

12.5 Entering text and numeric data

The spreadsheet in Figure 3.5 shows the sales figures for three different travel companies over a four-month period. Enter the data into the spreadsheet.

	A	B	C	D
1	MONTH	VOYAGE	GOING	TREKS
2	MAY	990	830	770
3	JUNE	550	880	220
4	JULY	330	660	700
5	AUGUST	400	550	820

Figure 3.5 *Spreadsheet data*

METHOD

1   Move to cell A1 and key in **MONTH**.
2   Move to cell B1 and key in **VOYAGE**.
3   Move to cell C1 and key in **GOING**.
4   Complete the worksheet in this way until it looks like Figure 3.5.

Note: When keying in numeric entries, you may find it quicker to use the numeric keypad on the right of the keyboard. Use the **Caps Lock** key to enter uppercase entries. Check entries when you have finished. Spreadsheets must be accurate or the results of any calculations will not be accurate. To correct an entry, click on: the cell, press: **Delete** and key in the entry again.

12.6   Entering simple formulae

Enter simple formulae to add up cell contents.

REMEMBER: Formulae must always begin with the = sign.

METHOD

1   Move to cell A6 and key in **TOTAL**.
2   First let Excel calculate the total sales figures for VOYAGE. These are displayed in cells B2, B3, B4 and B5. Move to cell B6 (where you want the answer to appear).

Information

Notice as you key in that the formula appears on the Formula bar. It may be too long to fit the cell but you can ignore this. Cell references can be in upper or lower case.

Key in:

=B2+B3+B4+B5 and press: **Enter**.

The answer 2270 appears in cell B6.

3   Now let Excel total the sales figures for GOING in the same way by keying in:

=C2+C3+C4+C5 and press: **Enter**

The answer 2920 appears in cell C6.

Your spreadsheet will now look like Figure 3.6.

	A	B	C	D
1	MONTH	VOYAGE	GOING	TREKS
2	MAY	990	830	770
3	JUNE	550	880	220
4	JULY	330	660	700
5	AUGUST	400	550	820
6	TOTAL	2270	2920	

Figure 3.6 Totalling column B and column C

12.7 Using the built-in Sum function

On a large business spreadsheet, you might need to add a huge number of cell contents and specifying each cell reference would not be practical. A quicker way to add up figures is by using one of Excel's built-in functions, **SUM**, to work out the formula as follows:

To produce a TOTAL for TREKS this time:

Move to cell D6 (where you want the answer to appear).
Key in **=SUM(D2:D5)** and press: **Enter**.

Information

The colon between the cell references in the formula above means 'to include all the cells in between D2 and D5'.

Your spreadsheet will now look like Figure 3.7.

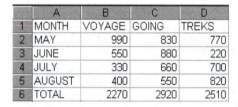

	A	B	C	D
1	MONTH	VOYAGE	GOING	TREKS
2	MAY	990	830	770
3	JUNE	550	880	220
4	JULY	330	660	700
5	AUGUST	400	550	820
6	TOTAL	2270	2920	2510

Figure 3.7 Totalling column D

Practice 12

Using the SUM function.

METHOD

1   Delete the Totals of VOYAGE (cell B6) and GOING (cell C6) by selecting them and pressing: **Delete**.
2   Add the Totals again, this time using the SUM function, in cell B6 **=SUM(B2:B5)** and in cell C6 **=SUM(C2:C5)**.

There is an even quicker way to add cell values using the toolbar button Σ **AutoSum**. To practise this, let's add up the totals for the three travel agents for each month.

METHOD

1 Move to cell E1 and key in **SALES**.
2 Move to cell E2, the cell where you want the total sales for MAY to appear.
3 Click on: the Σ **AutoSum** button. You will notice that a dotted line has appeared around cells B2 through to D2.

Information

In this example, Excel has automatically chosen the correct cells to add. Sometimes it may choose the wrong ones. If this happens you will need to select the cells you want manually. Click on the cell you want to start with, holding down the left mouse and dragging the dotted line across the correct cells. Be careful that you don't drag too far by mistake and include the cell where you want the answer to appear. The answer cell cannot be included in the formula. If you try to include in a formula the cell reference where you want the answer to appear, an error message will be displayed. Follow the instructions given in the error message.

4 Press: **Enter**.
5 The answer 2590 appears in cell E2.
6 Use this method to calculate the sales totals for JUNE, JULY and AUGUST.

Information

When adding sales for JULY, you will notice that Excel has mistakenly guessed that you now want to add the figures from above the cell and has placed the dotted line around cells E2 and E3. Move the highlight by clicking the first cell you want to add (B4) and dragging across to D4. Watch out for this.

If you have done everything correctly the totals will be as in Figure 3.8:

JUNE in cell E3   Total = 1650
JULY in cell E4   Total = 1690
AUGUST in cell E5   Total = 1770

	A	B	C	D	E
1	MONTH	VOYAGE	GOING	TREKS	SALES
2	MAY	990	830	770	2590
3	JUNE	550	880	220	1650
4	JULY	330	660	700	1690
5	AUGUST	400	550	820	1770
6	TOTAL	2270	2920	2510	

Figure 3.8 Sales figures for JUNE, JULY AND AUGUST

12.9 Saving the spreadsheet

METHOD

1 From the **File** menu, select: **Save As**. The Save As dialogue box appears (Figure 3.9).
2 Select the location where you want to save your file and key in **Sales** in the **File name** box.
3 Click on: **Save**.

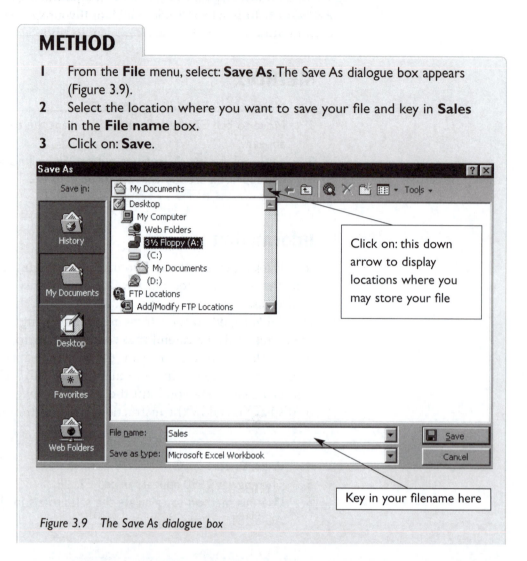

Figure 3.9 The Save As dialogue box

12.10 Printing spreadsheets

It is always wise to preview your spreadsheet before printing so you are sure it will print exactly what you want. This will save paper as well as effort.

METHOD

1 Click on: the ▱ **Print Preview** button.
2 Click on: the **Zoom** option to see your spreadsheet contents. Click on: **Zoom** again to return to default view.
3 If you are happy with the Print Preview, click on: **Print**. (You can change default options here if necessary.)
4 Click on: **OK**.

Information

Should you need to exit Print Preview at step 3, press: **Esc** *or* click on: **Close** to return to the spreadsheet.

Information

Printing in landscape
By default the spreadsheet will print a portrait display (the narrow edge at the top of the page). If you prefer, or if your spreadsheet does not fit across the page, you can change the display to landscape.

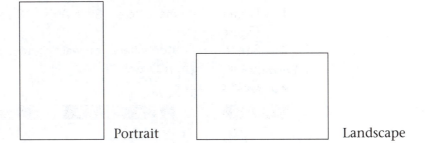

Portrait

Landscape

To do this from **Print Preview**, click on: **Setup**:
1   Click on: the **Page** tab, then on: the **Landscape** option button.
2   Click on: **OK**.

If not using Print Preview:
1   From the **File** menu, select: **Page Setup**.
2   Click on: the **Page** tab, then on: the **Landscape** option button.
3   Click on: **Print**.

12.11   Printing formulae

Information

It is sometimes useful to have a printout of the formulae used on your spreadsheet, or to see the formulae displayed on screen, so you can cross-reference for accuracy.

METHOD

To show formulae on your spreadsheet
1   With your spreadsheet on screen, from the **Tools** menu, select: **Options**.
2   Click on: the **View** tab (if not already selected); the Options dialogue box appears. Click on: the **Formulas** check box so that a tick appears in this box. Click on: **OK** (Figure 3.10).

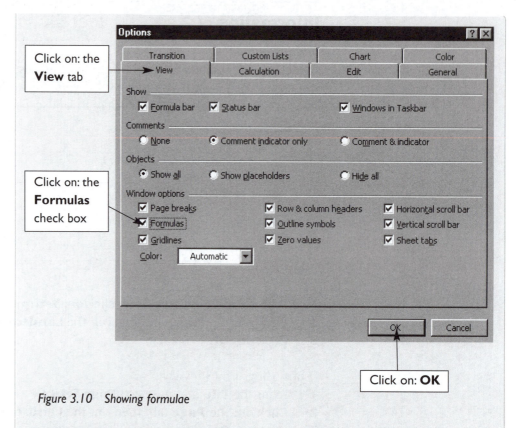

Click on: the **View** tab

Click on: the **Formulas** check box

Click on: **OK**

Figure 3.10   Showing formulae

Notice that the columns have widened to accommodate the formulae.

Information

Do not adjust the column widths because, when you take the 'show formulas' off, the cell widths will need altering again. For a quicker way to show formulae, press: **Ctrl** + ` (to the left of the number 1 key).

Check that the spreadsheet will fit on one page by using Print Preview (as above). If it fits, print as before. If it does not fit, check that it is in landscape by following the instructions above.

12.12   Changing the spreadsheet back so that numbers are displayed instead of formulae

METHOD

1   From the **Tools** menu, select: **Options**.
2   Click on: the **View** tab (if not already selected); click in: the **Formulas** check box so that the tick is removed. Click on: **OK**.

Information

A quick way to change back to the values display is to press: **Ctrl** + `.

12.13 Closing a spreadsheet file

Close the spreadsheet file. (In this case, do not save changes as you do not need to save the spreadsheet with the formulae displayed.)

METHOD

From the **File** menu, select: **Close**.

12.14 Exiting Excel

METHOD

Click on: the ☒ **Close** button in the top right-hand corner.

Task 12   Check

Practice 13

1   Load Excel.
2   Enter the following into the spreadsheet:

	A	B	C	D	E	F	G
1	PANCAKES						
2	TYPE	TUE	WED	THU	FRI	SAT	TOTAL
3	SPECIAL	10	12	14	12	10	
4	SUGAR	9	3	12	8	6	
5	LEMON	15	19	21	14	10	
6	SYRUP	22	26	21	0	4	
7	CHEESE	5	6	7	12	10	
8							

3   Enter a formula to calculate the total for the SPECIAL type only.
4   Save the spreadsheet with the name **pancakes**.
5   Print two copies, one showing the data, the other showing the formula used for the total.
6   Close the spreadsheet file.
7   Close Excel.

Practice 14

1   Load Excel.
2   Enter the following into the spreadsheet:

	A	B	C	D	E
1	DAY EXCURSIONS				
2	PLACE	TICKET	MEALS	OPTIONS	TOTAL
3	BATH	10.5	5	10	
4	BRISTOL	12	5	5	
5	YORK	25	15	12	
6	LONDON	15.55	10.75	14	
7	POOLE	8.5	5	0	
8					

3   Enter a formula to calculate the total for BATH only.

4   Save the spreadsheet with the name **trips**.

5   Print two copies, one showing the data, the other showing the formula used for the total.

6   Close the spreadsheet file.

Task 13   First steps with spreadsheets 2

This task follows on from task 12. It demonstrates the flexibility of spreadsheets.

When you have completed this task you will have learnt how to:
- reload a saved file
- change entries made to your spreadsheet
- delete a row or column
- replicate entries and formulae
- insert a new row or column
- recalculate data
- save the spreadsheet using a new filename.

13.1   Reloading a saved file

Reload the spreadsheet **Sales** saved in Task 12.

METHOD

1   With Excel loaded, click on: the ⊞ **Open** button; the Open dialogue box appears (Figure 3.11).

2   Select the location where your file is stored by clicking on: the down arrow.

3   Click on: the filename **Sales**.

4   Click on: **Open**.

Figure 3.12 Updated spreadsheet

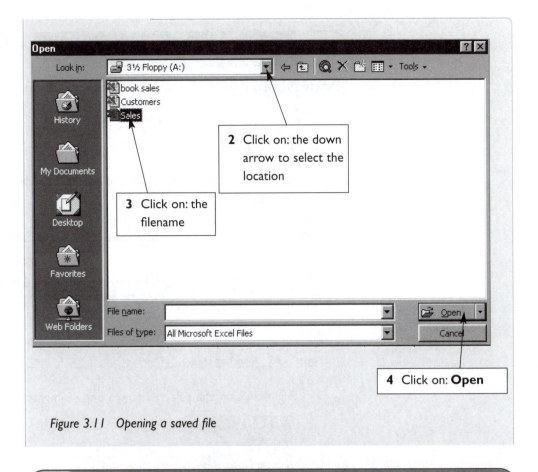

Figure 3.11   Opening a saved file

13.2   Changing entries made to your spreadsheet

Make the following changes:

The Sales figures for VOYAGE should be **850** (not **990**) in MAY and **470** (not **330**) in JULY.

METHOD

1   Move to cell B2 and key in: 850 and press: **Enter**.
2   Move to cell B4 and key in: 470 and press: **Enter**.

Information

Notice that the original figures are overwritten. Look what has happened to the Total for VOYAGE. You will see that the formula has been recalculated to give a new Total. The Sales figures for MAY and JULY in column E have also updated to reflect the changes made. This will usually happen; when you change cell contents within a spreadsheet, all the formulae referring to that cell will be automatically recalculated.

Your spreadsheet will now look like Figure 3.12.

	A	B	C	D	E
1	MONTH	VOYAGE	GOING	TREKS	SALES
2	MAY	850	830	770	2450
3	JUNE	550	880	220	1650
4	JULY	470	660	700	1830
5	AUGUST	400	550	820	1770
6	TOTAL	2270	2920	2510	
7					

Figure 3.12   Updated spreadsheet

13.3 Deleting a row or column

Delete the figure for JULY. Close the space (i.e. do not leave a blank row).

METHOD

1 Click in: the box to the left of the row to be deleted (i.e. row 4). Row 4 is highlighted (Figure 3.13).

Click here →

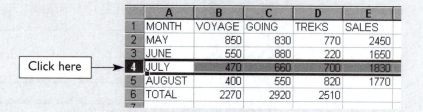

	A	B	C	D	E
1	MONTH	VOYAGE	GOING	TREKS	SALES
2	MAY	850	830	770	2450
3	JUNE	550	880	220	1650
4	JULY	470	660	700	1830
5	AUGUST	400	550	820	1770
6	TOTAL	2270	2920	2510	

Figure 3.13   Selecting a row

2 Right-click on: the selected row; a pop-up menu appears (Figure 3.14).

- ✂ Cut
- ▤ Copy
- ▤ Paste
- Paste Special...
- Insert...
- Delete...
- Clear Contents

Figure 3.14   Right-clicking displays a pop-up menu

3 Click on: **Delete**. The spreadsheet contents move up to occupy the empty space and the figures are recalculated to reflect the change (Figure 3.15).

	A	B	C	D	E
1	MONTH	VOYAGE	GOING	TREKS	SALES
2	MAY	850	830	770	2450
3	JUNE	550	880	220	1650
4	AUGUST	400	550	820	1770
5	TOTAL	1800	2260	1810	

Figure 3.15   Spreadsheet after deletion of the JULY row

The figures for GOING are no longer required; delete this column.

METHOD

1 Click in: the box at the top of the column to be deleted (i.e. C); column C is highlighted.
2 Right-click on: the selection; a pop-up menu appears.
3 Click on: **Delete**.

The spreadsheet now looks like Figure 3.16.

	A	B	C	D
1	MONTH	VOYAGE	TREKS	SALES
2	MAY	850	770	1620
3	JUNE	550	220	770
4	AUGUST	400	820	1220
5	TOTAL	1800	1810	
6				

Figure 3.16   Spreadsheet after deletion of the GOING column

13.4   Replicating entries and formulae

Replicate the formula used to calculate the TOTAL for TREKS so that the TOTAL for SALES is also calculated.

METHOD

1   Move to the cell in which the formula you want to copy is stored. In this case C5.
2   Point the mouse at the bottom right of this cell until a black cross ✚ appears, then, holding down the left mouse, drag across cell D5 (where you want the formula copied to). Release the mouse.
3   The spreadsheet now looks like Figure 3.17.

	A	B	C	D
1	MONTH	VOYAGE	TREKS	SALES
2	MAY	850	770	1620
3	JUNE	550	220	770
4	AUGUST	400	820	1220
5	TOTAL	1800	1810	3610

Figure 3.17   Spreadsheet after replication of formula

Information

If you make an error performing this procedure, Click on: the ↺ **Undo** button and try again.

13.5   Adding a new column and a new row

Adding a new column

Insert a new column headed TRAVELS after VOYAGE and before TREKS. Enter the following information: **MAY   600   JUNE   700   AUGUST   650**

METHOD

I   Click in: the box at the top of the column after where the new column is to appear (i.e. column C); column C is highlighted (Figure 3.18).

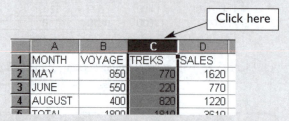

Figure 3.18   Selecting a column

2   Right-click on: the selection; a pop-up menu appears. Click on: **Insert** (Figure 3.19). An empty column appears.

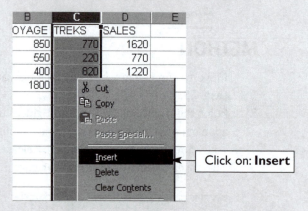

Figure 3.19   Inserting a column

3   Enter the new text and data shown above.

The spreadsheet now looks like Figure 3.20.

	A	B	C	D	E
1	MONTH	VOYAGE	TRAVELS	TREKS	SALES
2	MAY	850	600	770	2220
3	JUNE	550	700	220	1470
4	AUGUST	400	650	820	1870
5	TOTAL	1800		1810	5560
6					

Figure 3.20   Spreadsheet after addition of TRAVELS column and data

Calculate the Total for TRAVELS, using one of the quicker methods you have learnt. The Total is 1950.

Adding a new row

It has been decided to reinsert the figures for JULY. Insert a new row for JULY with the following information: **VOYAGE 470**, **TRAVELS 850**, **TREKS 700**.

METHOD

1   Click in: the box to the left of the row below where you want the new
    row to appear (i.e. row 4). Row 4 is highlighted (Figure 3.21).

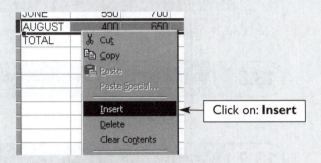

	A	B	C	D	E
1	MONTH	VOYAGE	TRAVELS	TREKS	SALES
2	MAY	850	600	770	2220
3	JUNE	550	700	220	1470
4	AUGUST	400	650	820	1870
5	TOTAL	1800	1950	1810	5560

Click here →

Figure 3.21   Adding a new row

2   Right-click on: the highlighted row; a pop-up menu appears (Figure
    3.22). Click on: **Insert**. An empty row appears.

JUNE	550	700
AUGUST	400	650
TOTAL		

- ✂ Cut
- ▤ Copy
- ▣ Paste
- Paste Special...
- Insert ← Click on: **Insert**
- Delete
- Clear Contents

Figure 3.22   Inserting a row

3   Enter the new text and data shown above.

Replicate the formula from cell E3 to produce a Total in cell E4 for JULY SALES.
The total is 2020.

13.6 Adding a new column or row to create new values

Insert a new column for JUSTGO after TREKS and before the SALES column
(see above, Figure 13.5). Enter the following data:

MAY   621   JUNE   890   JULY   700   AUGUST   440

Replicate the formula from D6 to give a Total value in cell E6 for JUSTGO.

Information

In Excel 2000, these figures (although at the end of the existing SUM cell
range) are automatically included in the SALES column figures. This did not
happen in earlier versions of Excel. Look out for this, as you may not always
want Excel to include new data in formulae.

METHOD

Follow the method in 13.5. The spreadsheet now looks like Figure 3.23.

	A	B	C	D	E	F
1	MONTH	VOYAGE	TRAVELS	TREKS	JUSTGO	SALES
2	MAY	850	600	770	621	2841
3	JUNE	550	700	220	890	2360
4	JULY	470	850	700	700	2720
5	AUGUST	400	650	820	440	2310
6	TOTAL	2270	2800	2510	2651	10231

Figure 3.23   Spreadsheet after adding the JUSTGO column

13.7   Saving the spreadsheet

Save your spreadsheet as Sales1.

13.8   Printing the spreadsheet

Print one copy on A4 paper.

13.9   Closing the file and exiting Excel

Close the file and exit Excel.

Task 13   Check

Practice 15

1   Load Excel.
2   Reload the spreadsheet **pancakes** saved in Task 12 Practice 13.
3   Delete the FRIDAY column.
4   Change the following entries: the SUGAR type for TUESDAY should be 9 not 10, the LEMON type for SATURDAY should be 100 not 10.
5   In the TOTAL column, replicate the formula for the total for the SUGAR type for all the other types.
6   Insert a new row in between the SPECIAL and SUGAR types with the type JAM. Enter the following data for JAM:

   Tue 6, **Wed 4**, **Thu 5**, **Sat 9**

7   Insert or replicate a formula for the total for this type.
8   Save the spreadsheet using the filename **pancakes1**.
9   Print one copy showing the data and one showing the formulae.
10   Close the spreadsheet file.

Practice 16

1   Load Excel.
2   Reload the file **trips** saved in Task 12 Practice 14.
3   Delete the row for LONDON.
4   In the TOTAL column, replicate the formula for the total of the BATH trip for all other trips.
5   Insert a new column for the discount available on each trip in between the columns OPTIONS and TOTAL, headed DISC. Enter the following values:

   BATH 5, **BRISTOL 2.5**, **YORK 3.75**, **POOLE 1**

   Note: If you look what has happened to the totals, you will see that they have increased. Excel has assumed that you wanted to add these values to the others. In fact, we need to take the discount values from the total. Always check that Excel is doing the correct calculations!

6   Create a formula for the total column for the BATH trip (i.e. the sum of ticket, meals and options minus discount) and replicate it for the other trips.
7   Save the spreadsheet using the name **trips with discounts**.
8   Print one copy showing the data and one showing the formulae used.
9   Close the spreadsheet file.

Task 14   Display features in Excel

There are many ways of displaying spreadsheet data. This task demonstrates how to align entries and display numeric entries in various formats.

> When you have completed this task you will have learnt how to:
> ● align cell entries
> ● widen columns
> ● use integer and decimal format to display numbers
> ● display in currency format.

14.1   Aligning cell entries

Information

When data is first entered, text is placed on the left of the cell and numbers line up on the right. Three toolbar buttons can be used to apply a new alignment to a range that is selected:

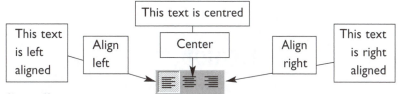

To align cell contents
1   Select the cells to be realigned.
2   Click on: the appropriate toolbar button.

Reload the spreadsheet **Sales1** saved at the end of Task 13. Display the headings: **MONTH**, **VOYAGE**, **TRAVELS**, **TREKS**, **JUSTGO** and **SALES** so that **MONTH** is left aligned and **VOYAGE**, **TRAVELS**, **TREKS**, **JUSTGO** and **SALES** are right aligned.

METHOD

The heading MONTH is already left aligned. To right align the other headings:

1   Select cells B1 to F1 (Figure 3.24).

	A	B	C	D	E	F
1	MONTH	VOYAGE	TRAVELS	TREKS	JUSTGO	SALES
2	MAY	850	600	770	621	2841
3	JUNE	550	700	220	890	2360

Figure 3.24   Cells selected to right align

2   Click on: the **Align Right** toolbar button.

Centring across cells

Insert a new row at the top of the spreadsheet and enter the heading **TRAVEL SALES** in cell A1. Centre this heading across the columns A to F.

METHOD

1   With the new row and heading entered, select: cells A1 to F1.
2   Click on: the ▦ **Merge and Center** button.

Note: Although this heading is positioned across the spreadsheet cells, its contents still reside in their original cell (i.e. A1). If you need to amend an entry that is centred, you must select its original cell only.

14.2   Changing column width

Information

By default, each column starts with a width of about nine numeric characters. You can adjust the column width so that it accommodates the entry within.

Change the heading **SALES** so that it becomes **MONTHLY SALES**.

METHOD

1   Move to cell F2.
2   Click the cursor in front of the **S** of **SALES** (Figure 3.25) on the formula bar and key in **MONTHLY** and a space. Press: **Enter**.

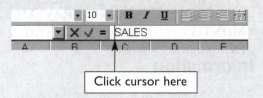

Click cursor here

Figure 3.25 Positioning the cursor to alter a heading

3 The entry is now too long to fit the cell. There are several ways to widen the column:

Information

Click on: the **Undo** toolbar button after trying each method so that you can practise.

---

a Position the cursor at the column border; a double arrow appears. Drag the right-hand edge of the column border (next to the column letter) to the right (Figure 3.26).

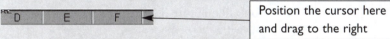

Position the cursor here and drag to the right

Figure 3.26 Changing column width

b Position the cursor as above and double-click the mouse (this action widens to fit the longest entry exactly).

c With the cell selected, from the **Format** menu, select: **Column, AutoFit Selection** (Figure 3.27).

Figure 3.27 Widening a column using the menus

4 Save the file.

Information

If a cell is filled with ####### characters, the column is not wide enough to display the numeric value held in that cell. Widen the cell as above to display the cell contents.

Information

An integer is a whole number (i.e. a number without decimal places). So numbers like 2, 6 and 10 are integers and 2.5, 4.8 and 1.5 are numbers with one decimal place (i.e. one number after the decimal point). 2.55 and 4.75 are numbers with two decimal places.

Enter a column headed **AVERAGE SALES** after the MONTHLY SALES column. Right align this heading and widen the cell to display this heading in full.

In cell G3, enter a formula to work out the AVERAGE SALES for MAY – i.e. MONTHLY SALES divided by 4 (as there are 4 companies). The formula is: =F3/4. (*Note*: You can also use the formula =AVERAGE(B3:E3).)

Replicate this formula to cells G4, G5, G6 and G7. The spreadsheet will now look like Figure 3.28.

	A	B	C	D	E	F	G
1				TRAVEL SALES			
2	MONTH	VOYAGE	TRAVELS	TREKS	JUSTGO	MONTHLY SALES	AVERAGE SALES
3	MAY	850	600	770	621	2841	710.25
4	JUNE	550	700	220	890	2360	590
5	JULY	470	850	700	700	2720	680
6	AUGUST	400	650	820	440	2310	577.5
7	TOTAL	2270	2800	2510	2651	10231	2557.75

Figure 3.28   Spreadsheet with the Average Sales column added

Notice that there are integers (whole numbers) in cells G4 and G5. Cell G6 has 1 decimal place (1 numeric character after the decimal point) and cells G3 and G7 have 2 decimal places (2 numeric characters after the decimal point).

Display the numeric data in the AVERAGE SALES column as integers (no decimal places).

METHOD

1   Select the column entries (i.e. cells G3 to G7).
2   Right-click: the highlighted area; a pop-up menu appears (Figure 3.29).

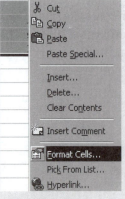

     Cut
     Copy
     Paste
     Paste Special...

     Insert...
     Delete...
     Clear Contents

     Insert Comment

     Format Cells...
     Pick From List...
     Hyperlink...

Figure 3.29   Formatting cells

3 From the menu, select: **Format Cells**; the Format Cells dialogue box is displayed (Figure 3.30).

4 Click on: the **Number** tab.

5 In the **Category** box, click on: **Number**.

6 In the **Decimal places** box, use the down arrow to set to zero (0).

4 Click on: the **Number** tab

5 Click on: **Number**

6 Set to the required number of decimal places

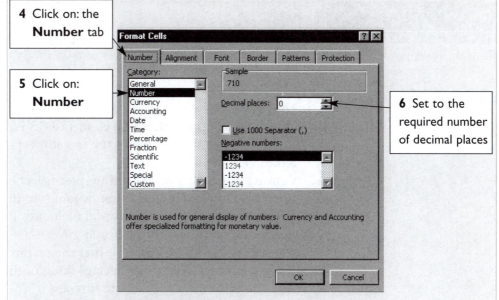

Figure 3.30   Format Cells dialogue box

7 Click on: **OK**.

The AVERAGE SALES column will now look like Figure 3.31.

AVERAGE SALES
710
590
680
578
2558

Figure 3.31   Average Sales figures displayed as integers

Follow the instructions above to display the numeric data in the **AVERAGE SALES** column to 2 decimal places (i.e. 2 places after the decimal point).

The AVERAGE SALES column should now look like Figure 3.32.

AVERAGE SALES
710.25
590.00
680.00
577.50
2557.75

Figure 3.32   Average Sales figures displayed with 2 decimal places

Information

You can also use the ⁺.⁰ .⁰⁰ / .⁰⁰ ⁺.⁰ **Increase and Decrease decimal** buttons. Select the cell to format first. Use the 💲 **Currency** button to give entries a £ symbol and 2 decimal places automatically. To reset the format to the default, from the **Format** menu, select: **Cells**, **Number** tab and **General**.

Save, print, close and exit

Save the spreadsheet with the name Sales2, print a copy, close the spreadsheet file and exit Excel.

Task 14)   Check

 Practice 17

1   Load Excel.
2   Reload the file **pancakes1** saved in Task 13 Practice 15.
3   Insert a new row at the top of the spreadsheet and enter the heading SALES W/E 22 June 2002.
4   Centre this heading across all the spreadsheet entries.
5   Align the days and total column headings to the right.
6   Centre all row headings below and including TYPE.
7   Add a new column with the heading AVERAGE SALES after the TOTAL column. Widen this column so that the text fits within it.
8   Insert a formula to generate average sales for the SPECIAL type and replicate this formula for all other types.
9   Display the average results as integers.
10   Save the spreadsheet as **pancakes2**.
11   Print two copies, one with values, the other with formulae.
12   Close the spreadsheet.

 Practice 18

1   Load Excel.
2   Reload the file **trips with discounts** saved in Task 13 Practice 16.
3   Change the word PLACE to DESTINATION. (Click in the cell, press: **Delete**. Key in the new text.)
4   Widen the column so that the DESTINATION text fits within it.
5   Change the heading DISC to DISCOUNT. Again widen the column to fit.
6   Display TICKET prices to 2 decimal places with no £ sign and all other monetary amounts as currency (i.e. with £ sign and 2 decimal places).
7   Save the spreadsheet as **trips with discounts1**.
8   Print a copy showing values.
9   Close the spreadsheet.

Task 15)   Recipe conversions

Most recipe books show recipes for four servings. This task shows you how to design a spreadsheet to work out a shopping list for a recipe to your own required number of servings. Depending on whether you are cooking less or more, you can then use the same spreadsheet time and again to work out exactly what you need, just by changing one value.

When you have completed this task you will have learnt how to:
●   understand relative and absolute cell references
●   add borders and shading to cells
●   change font and font attributes.

METHOD

1 Load Excel.
2 Enter the contents below on a new spreadsheet:

	A	B	C	D	E
1	Potato-topped Fish Pie				
2					
3	Ingredients	Unit of measure	Quantity for 4	Quantity for 1	Quantity for 14
4	Milk	ml	250		
5	Cod fillet	gram	450		
6	Oysters (optional)		12		
7	Potatoes	gram	900		
8	Butter	gram	50		
9					
10					
11	No of servings required				
12					

3 In column D, enter a formula for the quantity for one serving (i.e. =C4/4).
4 Replicate this for the other ingredients.
5 Next to the **No of servings required**, in column B, enter 14. (*Note*: You can enter any number you want, depending on how many servings you require.)
6 In cell E4, the formula to generate the amount of milk required for 14 servings is required. To do this cell B11 needs to be made absolute (see the information box below for an explanation of this). In cell E4, key in **=D4*** and then click the mouse on cell **B11**. With the cell active, press the **F4** key (at the top of the keyboard). You will notice that, on the formula bar, the formula looks like: **=D4*B11**. The $ symbols denote that the cell has an absolute reference. Press: **Enter**.
7 Replicate this formula for the other ingredients.
8 Save the spreadsheet with the name **fishpie** and print two copies, one with data, the other showing the formulae.

The spreadsheet will look like Figure 3.33.

	A	B	C	D	E
1	Potato-topped Fish Pie				
2					
3	Ingredients	Unit of measure	Quantity for 4	Quantity for 1	Quantity for 14
4	Milk	ml	250	62.5	875
5	Cod fillet	gram	450	112.5	1575
6	Oysters (optional)		12	3	42
7	Potatoes	gram	900	225	3150
8	Butter	gram	50	12.5	175
9					
10					
11	No of servings required	14			

Figure 3.33 The updated spreadsheet

The formulae will look like Figure 3.34.

	A	B	C	D	E
1	Potato-topped Fish Pie				
2					
3	Ingredients	Unit of measure	Quantity for 4	Quantity for 1	Quantity for 14
4	Milk	ml	250	=C4/4	=D4*B11
5	Cod fillet	gram	450	=C5/4	=D5*B11
6	Oysters (optional)		12	=C6/4	=D6*B11
7	Potatoes	gram	900	=C7/4	=D7*B11
8	Butter	gram	50	=C8/4	=D8*B11
9					
10					
11	No of servings required	14			
12					

Figure 3.34 Spreadsheet showing formulae and absolute cell references

Now, when you change the quantity in cell B11, the quantities in column E will change accordingly. (Of course, you will need to alter the heading in column E.)

You could add more columns to work out the costings too.

Information

Relative and absolute cell references
When replicating formulae, the cell references change to reflect their new position. A relative cell reference will change relatively to its position on the spreadsheet. By contrast, an absolute cell reference will not change even if it is replicated or moved to another part of the spreadsheet. If you need to make a cell reference absolute, add a $ sign in front of the column letter and another $ sign in front of the row number or press: **F4** when the cell is active when creating the formula.

In the example in Figure 3.34, if cell reference B11 is not made absolute, you will not be able to replicate the formula in cell E4 for the other ingredients. Try it to see what happens. You will notice that it tries to reference to cells relatively (i.e. B12, B13 and so on).

15.2 Adding borders and shading to cells

With any spreadsheet you can add borders and shading to make things clearer, more attractive or easier to read. Let's practise this here. Add borders and shading to the spreadsheet as shown below:

	A	B	C	D	E
1	Potato-topped Fish Pie				
2					
3	Ingredients	Unit of measure	Quantity for 4	Quantity for 1	Quantity for 14
4	Milk	ml	250	62.5	875
5	Cod fillet	gram	450	112.5	1575
6	Oysters (optional)		12	3	42
7	Potatoes	gram	900	225	3150
8	Butter	gram	50	12.5	175
9					
10					
11	No of servings required		14		
12					

Adding borders

1   Select the cell(s) that you want to have a border.
2   Click on: the down arrow of the **Borders** button. The borders
     selection appears (Figure 3.35).

Figure 3.35   Borders selection

3   Click on the relevant border.
4   Repeat for other bordered cells.

Adding shading

1   Select the cell(s) that you want to shade.
2   Click on: the down arrow of the **Fill Color** button. The colour
     selection appears (Figure 3.36).
3   Click on: a colour.
4   Repeat for the other cells to shade.

Figure 3.36   Adding shading to cells

15.3   Changing font and font attributes

1   Select the cells that you want to change. *Note:* To select non-adjacent cells,
     hold down the **Ctrl** key when selecting.
2   Use the toolbar buttons (as in Word) to change font and font attributes
     (i.e. size, bold and so on).

Save the spreadsheet as fishpie1 and print one copy.

15.5 Close and exit Excel

Close the file and exit Excel.

Task 16 Creating a household budget spreadsheet

There are endless spreadsheet layouts that you can use for a household budget depending on what you want to include. This task takes you through one possible layout. It uses separate sheets for each month within the same file (in Excel these sheets are collectively known as a *Workbook*). By selecting all the sheets and then entering the core data on one sheet, the data is automatically entered on all the selected sheets. This saves time and ensures that all the sheets are identical.

When you have completed this task you will have learnt how to:
● set up and work with separate sheets
● set up formulae before entering numeric data.

16.1 Creating separate sheets

Create sheets for a six-month period.

METHOD

1   Load Excel and have a look at the new spreadsheet window. You will notice that, by default, there are three sheet tabs at the bottom left of the window named Sheet1, Sheet2 and Sheet3 (Figure 3.37).

Figure 3.37   Default Sheet tabs

2   Rename the sheets as follows:

Right-click on: the **Sheet1** tab; a pop-up menu appears (Figure 3.38).

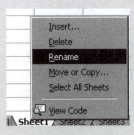

Figure 3.38   Renaming a sheet

Select: **Rename** and over key the selection with **Jan**.
Repeat for the other two sheet tabs naming them **Feb** and **Mar**.

3   Insert three (or nine if you want to create a complete year) new sheets as follows:

Right-click on: a sheet tab, from the pop-up menu (Figure 3.37); select: **Insert**.

Note: If the sheet has appeared in the wrong place, drag it using the mouse – i.e. point to the sheet you want to move, hold down the left mouse button and drag to the required position.

Rename the sheet as **Apr** as in step 2 above.
Repeat for the other new sheets, naming them **May** and **Jun**.

You now have six sheets as shown in Figure 3.39.

Figure 3.39   Sheet tabs created for six months

16.2   Selecting multiple sheets and entering data

Select all six sheets and enter the following data into the **Jan** sheet.

	A	B	C	D	E
1	MONTHLY ACCOUNTS				
2					
3	OUTGOINGS			INCOME	
4	Regular			Salary	
5	Rent/Mortgage			Overtime	
6	Council tax			Other	
7	Water charges			TOTAL MONTHLY INCOME	
8	Gas				
9	Electricity				
10	Internet				
11	Home Insurance			TOTAL CREDIT/DEBIT	
12	Car insurance				
13	TOTAL				
14					
15	Variable				
16	Food				
17	Petrol				
18	Bus/train fares				
19	Telephone				
20	Mobile				
21	Holidays				
22	Presents				
23	Car repairs				
24	TOTAL				
25					
26	TOTAL MONTHLY OUTGOINGS				
27					
28					

METHOD

1   Right-click on: the **Jan** sheet tab.
2   From the pop-up menu, select: **Select All Sheets**. The sheets tabs turn white and the Title bar now displays **Group**.
3   Enter the data into the **Jan** sheet. Format the cells as shown.

4 Save the spreadsheet with the filename **budget**. (*Note:* All six sheets are saved together in the same file.)

When you have finished, click on the other sheet tabs to view exactly the same entered data on those too.

16.3 Entering formulae

You are now ready to enter formulae that will do the calculations on the sheets.

METHOD

1 Right-click on: the **Jan** sheet tab and select all sheets as above.
2 Click in cell B13 and enter a formula to total the regular outgoings.

Note: There is no numeric data entered yet so the result will be 0.

3 Repeat for cells B24 and E7.
4 In cell C26, enter a formula to add the two Outgoings totals as follows:

   a Click in cell C26.
   b Click on: the **AutoSum** button.
   c Click on: cell B13. Hold down the **Ctrl** key and click on: cell B24.
   d Press: **Enter**.

Note: Since it is only two cells it would be just as quick to use =B13+B24.

5 In cell E11, enter a formula to calculate the difference between income and outgoings. The formulae will look similar to those in Figure 3.40.
6 Format these total cells to Currency by clicking on them (hold down the **Ctrl** key to select these non-adjacent cells all at once) and then click on: the **Currency** button.
7 Resave the file using the same filename as used previously.

	A	B	C	D	E
1	MONTHLY ACCOUNTS				
2					
3	OUTGOINGS			INCOME	
4	Regular			Salary	
5	Rent/Mortgage			Overtime	
6	Council tax			Other	
7	Water charges			TOTAL MONTHLY INCOME	=SUM(E4:E6)
8	Gas				
9	Electricity				
10	Internet				
11	Home Insurance			TOTAL CREDIT/DEBIT	=E7-C26
12	Car insurance				
13	TOTAL	=SUM(B5:B12)			
14					
15	Variable				
16	Food				
17	Petrol				
18	Bus/train fares				
19	Telephone				
20	Mobile				
21	Holidays				
22	Presents				
23	Car repairs				
24	TOTAL	=SUM(B16:B23)			
25					
26	TOTAL MONTHLY OUTGOINGS		=SUM(B13,B24)		

Figure 3.40 Formulae entered

The six monthly sheets are now ready for your data. Now that you have set up the formulae, calculations will be carried out automatically.

16.4 Print

Print copies of the sheets for Jan and Feb showing the formulae used.

16.5 Close and exit Excel

Close the file and exit Excel.

Information

A more comprehensive budget spreadsheet could look like Figure 3.41.

MONTHLY ACCOUNTS

		OUTGOINGS			INCOME	
Accommodation		Transport			Salary	
Rent/Mortgage		Bus fares			Gifts	
Council tax		Train fares			Interest on savings	
Water charges		Car repayment			other	
Gas		Car insurance			TOTAL MONTHLY INCOME	£ -
Electricity		Car tax				
Telephone (landline)		Petrol				
Mobile		Repairs/servicing			TOTAL CREDIT/DEBIT	£ -
Internet		TOTAL	£ -			
Insurance						
Misc		Other regular outgoings				
TOTAL	£ -	Personal loan				
		Credit card repayments				
Food		Pension plan				
Supermarket		Personal travel insurance				
Other groceries		Other				
Meals out		TOTAL	£ -			
TOTAL	£ -					
		Other expenses				
		Nights out (cinema, theatre etc)				
		Holidays				
		Presents				
		TOTAL	£ -			
TOTAL MONTHLY OUTGOINGS	£ -					

Figure 3.41   A more comprehensive budget spreadsheet layout

Task 17   Using Excel for data storage

Although Excel is used for tasks that involve calculations, it can also be used for data storage. You can set up, for example, an inventory of your music CD collection, your stamp collection or toys in a playgroup toy library. Data stored in this way is referred to as a *database*. There are dedicated database applications, such as Microsoft Access, that have all the frills but Excel can be used for a simple database. This task creates a database of household appliances. It is used to demonstrate what you can do with the data (i.e. sort it into a specific order or search for an item). You can add, delete or amend data as necessary. Of course this database is very small but you will be able to discover the potential for larger databases when it is not feasible to skim for items just by looking.

When you have completed this task you will have learnt how to:
- set up a simple database
- sort data
- search for data
- add, delete or amend data.

17.1 Creating a database in Excel

METHOD

I   Load Excel and enter the following data into a new spreadsheet.

	A	B	C	D	E	F	G
1	Appliance	Make	Model	Serial Number	Where purchased	Date purchased	Guarantee period (yrs)
2	Cooker	Easycook	E27	EC821900	Meteor	12/02/02	3
3	Fridge	Coldasice	Cube2	CA294112	Murrys	16/06/99	5
4	TV	Screened	Hi6	T21085532	Meteor	23/07/02	3
5	Washing machine	Whirly	W3	W32100000	Jenkins Ltd	03/07/01	5
6	Lawnmower	Hovery	L65	QLI29111	Homechase	04/04/97	1
7	Video reorder	Framed	CU2	G0000222	Meteor	23/07/02	3

2   Save the file with the name **appliances**.

Note: When entering previously entered data (e.g. Meteor), Excel will automatically complete the entry for you. You can turn this option off as follows:

a   From the **Tools** menu, select: **Options**.
b   With the **Edit** tab selected, click in the: **Enable AutoComplete for cell values** box to remove the tick.
c   Click on: **OK**.

Information

Structure of databases
Databases consist of records and fields. In this database there are six records (in rows) – i.e. Cooker, Fridge, etc. Each record here has seven fields (in columns), i.e. Appliance, Make, etc. Therefore row 2 represents the record for Cooker.

17.2 Sorting the data

Sort the data into alphabetical order of Appliance.

METHOD

1   Click in: cell A1.
2   From the **Data** menu, select: **Sort**. The Sort box is displayed (Figure 3.42).

Figure 3.42   The Sort box

3   In the **Sort by** box, select: **Appliance**. Ensure that the **Ascending** option button is selected.
4   In the **My list has** section, click in: the **Header row** option button. (*Note*: If you do not do this, the headers may be sorted with the appliances!)
5   Click on: **OK**.

Information

You can sort on any of the fields (e.g. Where purchased, Date purchased and so on), by selecting the appropriate field from the drop-down menu (click on the down arrow) of the **Sort by** box. You can also sort on more than one field by selecting from the **Then by** boxes. The Sort by option is sorted first, then the option in the first **Then by** box is sorted in relation to the first sort.

17.3   Searching for data

Search for all appliances purchased from Meteor.

METHOD 1

Using a Data Form
1   From the **Data** menu, select: **Form**.
2   The **Sheet1** Data Form box is displayed (Figure 3.43).

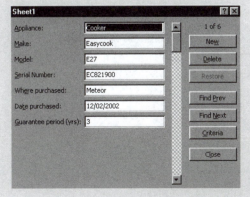

Figure 3.43   Data Form

3 Click on: the **Criteria** button.

4 Enter the text **Meteor** into the **Where purchased** box.

5 Use the **Find Next**, **Find Prev** buttons to view all appliance details purchased from Meteor.

Information

You can use the Data Form to add new records to the database, delete or amend them. You can also add, delete or amend records directly on the spreadsheet itself.

METHOD 2

Using AutoFilter

1 From the **Data** menu, select: **Filter**, **AutoFilter**.

2 Arrows appear on the field headings row.

3 Click on the down arrow of the **Where purchased** field. A list of entries in that field is displayed (Figure 3.44).

4 Select: **Meteor**.

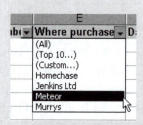

Figure 3.44   Entries in Where purchased field

5 The records of appliances purchased at Meteor are displayed (Figure 3.45).

Appliance	Make	Mode	Serial Numbe	Where purchase	Date purchase	Guaran
Cooker	Easycook	E27	EC821900	Meteor	12/02/02	
TV	Screened	Hi6	T21085532	Meteor	23/07/02	
Video reorder	Framed	CU2	G0000222	Meteor	23/07/02	

Figure 3.45   Selected records displayed

Note: Excel has hidden the rows that do not display the criteria. To redisplay all data:

From the **Data** menu, select: **Filter, Show All**.

17.4   Close and exit Excel

Close the file and exit Excel.

Action	Keyboard	Mouse	Right-mouse menu	Menu
Absolute cell reference	Add $ sign in front of the cell reference column letter and in front of the cell reference row number or press: **F4**			
Align cell entries	Select cells to align			
		Click: the relevant button: ▤ ▤ ▤ ▤	**Format Cells**	**F**ormat, **C**ells
			Select: the **Alignment** tab Select from the **Horizontal**: drop-down menu as appropriate	
Autofill	Select the first cell, drag the **Fill Handle** across the cells			
Bold text	Select the cells to embolden			
	Ctrl + B	Click: the **B** **Bold** button	**Format Cells**	**F**ormat, **C**ells
			Select: the Font tab Select: Bold from the Font style: menu	
Borders and shading	Select the cells that you want to add a border/shading to			
		Click on the down arrow of the ▭ ▾ **Borders** or ▨ ▾ **Fill Color** button. Select: the border/colour you require	**Format Cells, Border/ Patterns** tab	**F**ormat, **C**ells, **Border/Patterns** tab
Capitals (blocked)	**Caps Lock** (press again to remove)			
Close a file	**Ctrl + W**	Click: the ☒ **Close** button		**F**ile, **C**lose
Columns, add	Select the column following the one where you want the new column to appear by clicking on the column ref box (at top of column)			
			Insert	**Insert, Columns**
Columns, change width		Drag the column border [C ↔ D] to fit the widest entry	Select the column(s) by clicking (and dragging) on the column ref box (at top of column)	
			Column Width Key in the width you want	**F**ormat, **C**olumn, **W**idth Key in the width you want *or* **F**ormat, **C**olumn, **AutoFit Selection**
Columns, delete	Select the column you want to delete by clicking on the column ref box (at top of column)			
	Delete		**Delete**	**E**dit, **D**elete
Currency symbols		Click: the ▥ **Currency** button for UK currency		**Format, Cells, Number, Category, Currency,** select: symbol to use

Action	Keyboard	Mouse	Right-mouse menu	Menu
Decimal places		Click: the Increase Decimal button to increase the number of decimal places	Format Cells	Format, Cells
		Click: the Decrease Decimal to decrease the number of decimal places	Select the Number tab Click: Number in the Category: menu Select the number of decimal places you need	
Enter text	Click: in the cell where you want text to appear Key in: the text Press: **Enter**			
Enter numeric data	Click: in the cell where you want text to appear Key in: the data Press: **Enter**			
Enter formulae	Click: in the cell where you want text to appear Key in: = followed by the formula Press: **Enter**			
Exit the program		Click: the Close button		**File, Exit**
Fit to page				**File, Page Setup, Fit to (1) Page**
Formulae, functions	Click on the cell where the result is required Use: **=SUM(cell ref:cell ref)** for adding a range of cells *or* Click: Σ **AutoSum** button Click and drag over the cell range Press: **Enter** Use: **=AVERAGE(cell ref:cell ref)** to find the average value in a range of cells			
Formulae, operators	+ add - subtract * multiply / divide			
Formulae, show	**Ctrl + `**			**Tools, Options, View** Under **Window options**, select **Formulas** so that a tick appears
Formulae, print	Ensure the formulae are showing			
				File, Page Setup, Page tab, **Landscape** *or* **File, Page Setup, Page** tab Under Scaling, select **Fit to 1 page wide** and **1 page tall**
Help	**F1**			**Help** **Microsoft Excel Help**
	Shift + F1			**Help, What's This?**

Action	Keyboard	Mouse	Right-mouse menu	Menu
Integers (whole numbers)		Click: the .00 +.0 **Decrease Decimal** button until you have reduced the number of decimal places to zero	**Format Cells**	**Format, Cells**
			Select the **Number** tab Click: **Number** in the **Category** menu Change the number of decimal places to zero	
Move around	Use the cursor keys	Click where you want to move to		
Move to top of document	**Ctrl + Home**			
Move to end of document	**Ctrl + End**			
New file	**Ctrl + N**	Click: the 🗋 **New** button		**File, New**
Open an existing file	**Ctrl + O**	Click: the 📂 **Open** button		**File, Open**
	Select: the drive required Select: the filename Click: **Open**			
Page Setup	From the **File** menu, select: **Page Setup** Choose from **Margins, Paper Size, Paper Source, Layout**			
Print file	**Ctrl + P** Select: the options you need Press: **Enter**	Click: the 🖨 **Print** button		**File, Print** Select the options you need and click: **OK**
Print in Landscape	From the **File** menu, select: **Page Setup** Click: the **Page** tab Select: **Landscape** Click: **OK**			
Print selected cells only	Select the cells to print			
	Ctrl + P			**File, Print**
	Select: **Selection**			
	Click: **OK**			
Print preview		Click: the 🔎 **Print Preview** button		**File, Print Preview**
Remove text emphasis	Select text to be changed			
	Ctrl + B (remove bold) **Ctrl + I** (remove italics) **Ctrl + U** (remove underline)	Click: the appropriate button: **B** *I* <u>U</u>	**Format Cells**	**Format, Cells**
			Select the **Font** tab Click: **Regular** in the **Font Style**: menu	
Replicate (copy) formulae	Select: the cell with the formula to be copied Drag the mouse from the bottom right corner of the cell over the cells to copy to Release mouse			

Action	Keyboard	Mouse	Right-mouse menu	Menu
Restore deleted input	**Ctrl + Z**	Click: the ↩ **Undo** button		**E**dit, **U**ndo
Rows, add	Select the row by clicking in the row ref box (at side of row) below the one where you want the new row to appear				
			Insert	**Insert**, **Rows**
Rows, delete	Select the row by clicking in the row ref box (at side of row) below the one that you want to delete				
			Delete	**E**dit, **D**elete
Save	**Ctrl + S**	Click: the 💾 **Save** button		**F**ile, **S**ave
	If you have not already saved the file you will be prompted to specify the directory and to name the file If you have already done this, Excel will automatically save it				
Save using a different name or to a different directory				**F**ile, Save **A**s
	Select: the appropriate drive and change the filename if relevant Click: **Save**				
Search for data				**D**ata, **F**orm *or* **D**ata, **F**ilter
Select cells	Click and drag across cells				
Select non-adjacent cells	Select the first cell(s), hold down: **Ctrl** and click the others				
Remove selection	Click in any white space				
Sheets, add				**I**nsert, **W**orksheet
change	Click on: appropriate sheet tab				
delete			Right-click on: Sheet tab. Select: **D**elete	
rename			Right-click on: sheet tab. Select: **R**ename	
select multiple	Right-click on: one sheet: select: **Select All Sheets**				
Sort data				**D**ata, **S**ort
Spell check	Move cursor to top of document				
	F7	Click: the ✓ **Spelling** button		**T**ools, **S**pelling

Action	Keyboard	Mouse	Right-mouse menu	Menu
Text formatting: font, size, colour, italicise, embolden, orientation	Select cell(s) to format			
	Ctrl + B embolden **Ctrl + I** italicise **Ctrl + U** underline	Click: the relevant toolbar button on the formatting toolbar	**Format Cells, Font** tab For orientation: **Alignment** tab	**Format, Cells, Font** tab For orientation: **Alignment** tab
Toolbar, modify				**View, Toolbars, Customize**
Undo	**Ctrl + Z**	Click: the ↶ **Undo** button		**Edit, Undo**
Zoom		Click: the 100% ▾ **Zoom** button		**View, Zoom**

COPYING, CUTTING AND PASTING CELLS
Select cell(s) to copy/cut
Using Cut/Copy and Paste
Click: the **Cut/Paste** button. Select where you want to cut/copy to. Click: the **Paste** button.

Using drag and drop
Copy: Hold down: **Ctrl** and drag to new position.
Cut: Drag to new position.

USING AUTOFILL
If the cell contains a number, date or time period that can extend in a series, by dragging the fill handle of a cell you can copy that cell to other cells in the same row or column. The values are incremented. For example, if the cell contains MONDAY, you can quickly fill in other cells in a row or column with TUESDAY, WEDNESDAY and so on.

1 Key in and enter the first label or, if numeric, key in and enter the first 2 numbers.
2 Select the cell(s) containing the label or numbers you entered.
3 Move the mouse over the bottom right corner of the selected cell(s).
4 Press and hold down the left mouse and drag over the cells you want to include in the series.

Have you heard of terms like 'surfing the net', 'going online' and 'sending email'? And what about all those 'www dot blah dot blah' addresses that you see and hear everywhere? The tasks that follow bring an understanding to what all the fuss is about. It really is no surprise that everyone is talking about the Internet. It has revolutionised the way we communicate with others and the way we access information of all kinds. If you have the technology to enable you to do the tasks in this chapter, you will begin to realise for yourself the absolute wonder of modern communications.

Task 18 provides explanations and cuts through some of the jargon. Tasks 19 and 20 cover using the Internet to search for specific information and organising what you have found. Tasks 21 to 25 address using electronic communications (email).

Note: Computer viruses are often spread through computer communications so you should be aware of this. Viruses are small programs that are written by people with the know-how who want to play a joke or cause widespread damage to computer systems. A virus is so called because it can be passed on from one computer to another. Computer viruses do not infect humans! A virus hides itself so that you do not notice it is there until strange things start happening to your computer. It might be something very simple (e.g. a message is displayed or a tune is played), or it could be something much more serious resulting in all your files being destroyed. They do not cause any physical damage.

It is best to try to protect your computer from being infected by a virus in the first place. You can do this by using *antivirus utility programs*. These can alert you to a virus and can often remove it. They are a good 'insurance' investment. They must be updated regularly to cope with any new viruses.

Task 18 ## The Internet, the world wide web and email

This task explains some modern communications terms you may have heard but are not quite sure what they mean.

When you have completed this task you will have learnt how to understand the terms Internet, world wide web and email.

18.1 What is the Internet?

The *Internet* is made up of interconnected computer networks all over the world that send, receive and store information. An individual with a computer and the relevant communications equipment can gain access to this network by subscribing to an *Internet service provider* (*ISP*) so that you can connect to the Internet as often or as seldom as you like (or can afford). Large companies, educational establishments and government offices have their own arrangements and they are usually connected to the Internet all the time.

18.2 What is the world wide web?

The *world wide web* (*www* or *web* for short) is one of the services run on the Internet. It contains millions of websites – linked pages of words that sometimes include pictures, sounds and graphics. You can explore all these sites using a web browser (an application such as Internet Explorer). Web pages contain *hyperlinks* to other web pages and other websites so that users can plot their route through depending on their area of interest. Moving through sites on the web in this way is known as *surfing*.

The number of websites is growing at a phenomenal rate. Each website is created and managed by an organisation or individual and each has its own unique address so that you can locate it. Websites are stored on computers connected to the Internet. In fact, with a little know-how, anyone can create a website, and ISPs usually provide the facility and storage space to host one. Websites come and go and are constantly being updated. As a result, what you see on a site one day could be quite different from what you see the following week.

Note: The web addresses and screenshots of sites used in this book were correct at the time of writing but may have changed by the time you access them.

Websites are usually presented in an interesting and attractive way to encourage you to spend time exploring them. A wide selection of sites provide information on almost every subject imaginable. You can find information such as train times, weather forecasts, the latest news or you can look things up as you might in an encyclopaedia. You can shop on the web – order your groceries to be delivered to your home without stepping outside, or just browse through the latest items for sale in your favourite store. Once you get started you may want to make a note of all those www addresses that you see. As well as all this, you can also gain access to newsgroups and chatrooms where you are able to join in with discussions on topics that interest you.

18.3 What is email?

Electronic mail (*email*) is a method of sending messages between computers located anywhere in the world. You exchange the electronic equivalent of letters, faxes, pictures and sound with anyone who has an email address. Some organisations have their own internal email systems and are also connected to the Internet to send and receive email locally and internationally. A typical home user has an ISP that allocates them an email address so that people know where to send their messages. Email is a quick and efficient means of communication. It has the advantage that you can send and receive your messages when you choose (unlike telephone communication) and is cheaper because calls are charged at local rates (and sometimes even free!). To save money, you can compose and read messages when you are disconnected from the telephone line. In addition, you will usually be informed if your message has failed to reach its destination. Email messages (and any files transmitted with them) can be saved and edited by the recipient, whether text or graphics, to produce new documents.

18.4 Counting the cost

When you are connected to the Internet, all calls are charged at local telephone rates. The deal that you have with your ISP will determine how much your surfing will cost. Some ISPs offer some hours free but technical support, when you need it, could be expensive. They all have their individual deals (these are changing all the time) so it is worth shopping around for the best to suit your particular needs.

If you pay for your calls, it is worth waiting for the times of day when it is cheap rate, or weekends. Some phone companies have a minimum three-minute charge so it is better to be connected for the full three minutes than make three one-minute connections. Keep a note of how long you are spending *online* (connected). Read web pages *offline* (when not connected) and compose and read emails offline too. Once you have learnt the basics, use short cut keys to save time. It is surprising how the phone bill can mount up when you become too engrossed with surfing! If you plan to use the Internet a lot, ensure you add the Internet number to your low-cost options with your telephone provider.

Task 18 Check

Describe the following (briefly):

the Internet	
the world wide web	
Email	
the costs involved when accessing the Internet	

Task 19 Using the web

This task shows you how to launch your browser (this book uses Internet Explorer), connect to the Internet and start searching for information on the web.

Note: Methods of connecting to the Internet have the same principles but may vary depending on your particular communications equipment and ISP.

When you have completed this task you will have learnt how to:
- connect to the Internet
- load a web browser
- access web addresses
- change the display
- search for specific information
- save and print information
- exit a web browser.

19.1 Loading Internet Explorer

METHOD

From the **Start** menu, select: **Programs**, **Internet Explorer** or click on the 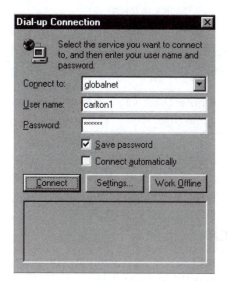 **Launch Internet Explorer Browser** icon on the **Taskbar**.

Information

If you are not already connected to the Internet, a dialogue box similar to the one below will be displayed. Key in your **User name** and **Password** and click on: **Connect**. Passwords are used to prevent unauthorised access. Always choose one that is not easy for others to guess.

When you are connected the icon appears on the Taskbar. To disconnect, right-click on the icon and select: **Disconnect**.

Either method will result in the Internet Explorer window being displayed (Figure 4.1).

Note: The web page displayed is determined by the setup of your computer (see Task 20). Toolbar buttons are labelled in Figure 4.2.

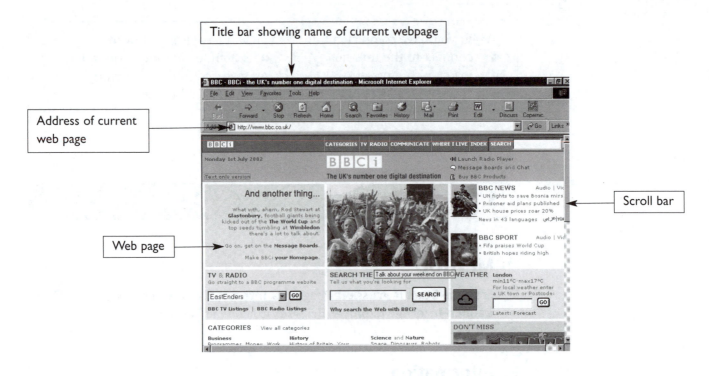

Title bar showing name of current webpage

Address of current web page

Scroll bar

Web page

Figure 4.1 Internet Explorer window displaying the BBC website home page

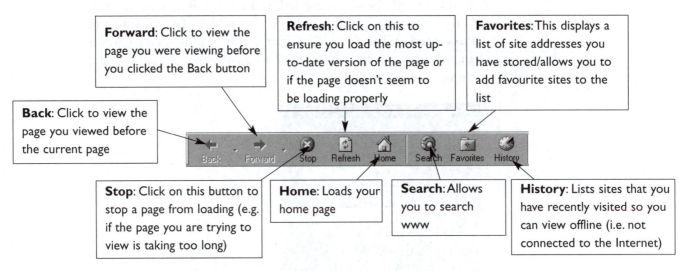

Forward: Click to view the page you were viewing before you clicked the Back button

Refresh: Click on this to ensure you load the most up-to-date version of the page *or* if the page doesn't seem to be loading properly

Favorites: This displays a list of site addresses you have stored/allows you to add favourite sites to the list

Back: Click to view the page you viewed before the current page

Stop: Click on this button to stop a page from loading (e.g. if the page you are trying to view is taking too long)

Home: Loads your home page

Search: Allows you to search www

History: Lists sites that you have recently visited so you can view offline (i.e. not connected to the Internet)

Figure 4.2 Internet Explorer toolbar buttons

Information

Web pages vary in length. If some of the web page is out of view, use the scroll bar to reveal the remainder.

If you find the web pages difficult to read (i.e. text is too small or too large), you can adjust the size of the text. To do this, from the **View** menu, select: **Text Size**. Make your selection as appropriate. The default setting is **Medium**.

19.2 What is a web address?

A *website* is a collection of pages on the web owned by an individual or organisation. The first page of a website is the *home page*. Every web page has a unique address. This is known as a **URL** (**U**niform **R**esource **L**ocator). It usually begins with 'http://www' (http stands for *HyperText Transfer Protocol* and tells the web browser that it is looking for a web page). Most modern browsers have 'http://' stored so you can usually ignore the http part and start at 'www'. Here are some addresses to examine (the first accesses the page displayed in Figure 4.1):

http://www.bbc.co.uk
http://www.f1-live.com
http://www.nhm.ac.uk

The text after the www shows the *domain name* – the organisation's name, e.g. BBC, f1 (Formula 1) and nhm (Natural History Museum); the type of site, e.g. .co and .com are commercial companies, .ac is an academic community, and the country, e.g. uk is United Kingdom.

Note: The dots are important in a web address and the address must be spelt correctly. Sometimes addresses are longer because they include the pathname (an exact location within the website), e.g.:

www.bbc.co.uk/weather/worldweather/europe/index.shtml

19.3 Displaying a given web page

Display the following web page:

http://www.nhm.ac.uk

METHOD

1 Key in the web address in the address bar; press: **Enter** or click on the
   ⟳ Go **Go to** button.

2 The home page of the Natural History Museum website is displayed (Figure 4.3).

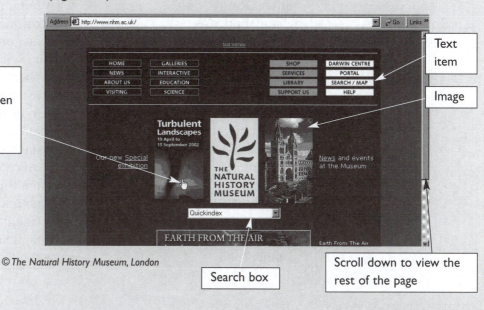

If the mouse pointer turns into a hand when hovering over, it denotes a hyperlink

Text item

Image

© The Natural History Museum, London

Search box

Scroll down to view the rest of the page

Figure 4.3   An example web page

Web pages have links (called *hyperlinks*) that you can click on to take you to other places within the current page, current site or to other websites. Links can take the form of underlined text, text in a different colour or they can be image links. When you hover over a link the mouse pointer (usually) turns into a hand. The home page of the Natural History Museum site (displayed in Figure 4.3) has text and image links.

Follow one of the links on the Natural History Museum home page to find out specific information (e.g. what galleries are there? What is new?).

METHOD

1   Click on the link. Another page of the site is displayed. Notice that the address and Title bar have changed to reflect that you are viewing another page.

2   Collect the information you are looking for. Return to the original page by clicking on the [Back] **Back** button.

Note: If you click on the down arrow of the **Back** button, if you have visited several pages, you can go back several pages at once. You will notice that the previously viewed pages may load quicker because your computer has temporarily stored their contents.

Information

A number of popular website addresses you may like to visit are given here.

All Recipes	www.allrecipes.com
Angela Bessant's website	www.bessant.co.uk
Art Guide	www.artguide.org
BBC Health	www.bbc.co.uk/health
BBC News	news.bbc.co.uk
Britannica	www.britannica.com
Coronation Street	www.coronationstreet.co.uk
Dictionary.com	www.dictionary.com
Do It Yourself.com	doityourself.com
EastEnders	www.bbc.co.uk/eastenders
Fishing	www.fishing.co.uk
Football 365	www.football365.com
Information Britain	www.information-britain.co.uk
International Movie Database	www.imdb.com
ITN Online	www.itn.co.uk
Multimap	www.multimap.com
National Gallery	www.nationalgallery.org.uk
Scoot Cinema Guide	www.cinema.scoot.co.uk
Scrabble	www.mattelscrabble.com/en/home.html
Simply Food	www.simplyfood.com

The Guardian	www.newsunlimited.co.uk
The History Channel UK	www.historychannel.com
The Mirror	www.mirror.co.uk
The Times	www.the-times.co.uk

19.5 Displaying/not displaying images

Information

Since image files are quite large, it is quicker to load a web page when you do not load the images contained in it. On many websites, you can select text-only versions but you can also set up your browser so that it does not display images.

Using browser settings, load the Natural History Museum home page (as above) without images. Then change the settings back to load the page with images.

METHOD

1   From the **Tools** menu, select: **Internet Options**.
2   Click on: the **Advanced** tab.
3   In the **Multimedia** section, click in the boxes next to **Show pictures**, **Play videos**, **Play animations** so that there are no ticks.
4   Click on: **Apply** and then on: **OK**.
5   Key in the Natural History Museum address.
6   The Natural History Museum home page is displayed without images.

Re-loading with images
7   Follow steps 1 to 5 again, this time placing ticks where they were removed.

Click on: **Refresh** button to redisplay the page with images.

19.6 Searching for information

There are many ways that you can find information on the web:

- If you know the web address of the site where you can find the information, go straight to the site by keying in the address and use hyperlinks to navigate through the site (or use the site's search box if it has one).
- Using Internet Explorer's **Search** button enables you to key in a word(s) (known as a **key** word) or phrase. It then uses a search engine that will look for the key word(s) on a database of websites. A search engine looks like a normal web page with a form to enter key words that you are looking for. It runs a program that searches its own database (an up-to-date list of web sites) and provides you with a list of 'hits' – i.e. sites that contain the keyword(s).

- Using a chosen search engine. There are many search engine sites. You will find that a particular search engine usually finds what you are looking for or/and you find it easy to use. Popular search engines include:

  http://www.google.co.uk
  http://www.altavista.com
  http://www.ask.co.uk

- Using a search directory. A search directory sets out information in subject categories. This is useful if you are conducting a broad search. One common search directory is Yahoo http://www.yahoo.com. Other search directories include:

  Lycos http://www.lycos.com
  or for specific UK results from Lycos http://www.ukplus.co.uk

  What's New http://www.whatsnew.com

  Find sites where you can look up train times using the different search methods. Compare the different methods as you progress (i.e. time taken, usefulness of results, ease of use).

19.7 Using the Search button

METHOD

1 Click on the Search button.
2 Key **train times** into the **Search** box and enter it by clicking on: **Search** (Figure 4.4).

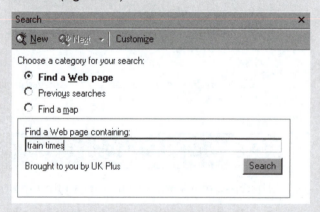

Figure 4.4   *Finding information using Search*

3 The search revealed numerous possible links (Figure 4.5). They are listed with the most relevant at the top.
4 Read the summaries to decide which are the most relevant for your purposes and follow the hyperlinks for information.

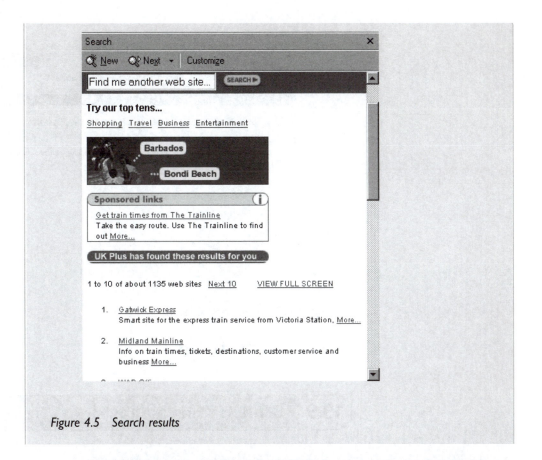

Figure 4.5   Search results

19.8   Using a search engine

METHOD

1   Access the Google website (http://www.google.co.uk).
2   Key **train times** into the **Search** box, click in the: **pages from the UK** button and enter it by clicking on **Google Search** (Figure 4.6).
Note: If you click on: **I'm Feeling Lucky,** you will be taken straight to (what Google believes) is the most relevant site.

Figure 4.6   Using a search engine

3   The search resulted in those things shown in Figure 4.7.

Figure 4.7   Search engine results

4   Follow the hyperlinks.

19.9   Using a search directory

METHOD

I   Log on to the Yahoo site. Figure 4.8 shows some of the site's categories.

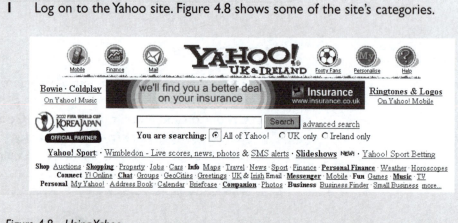

Figure 4.8   Using Yahoo

2   Click on hyperlinks that you think may contain the information you are looking for (e.g. **Travel**).

Try to find out train times travelling from Milton Keynes Central to Birmingham New Street leaving at approximately 09.00 and returning at 16.00 on Wednesdays.

19.10   Refining searches

As you can see from the previous exercises, searches can result in a huge number of possibly useful sites. You will be glad to know that you can refine your searches so that the results are more relevant. This is achieved by using (what are termed) logical operators – i.e. AND, NOT (or their equivalents AND, +, &; NOT, -) and OR. Different search engines have slightly different rules about how you enter searches with logical operators.

Using AND

Use AND or one of the symbols when searching for more than one word. Results will list sites that contain all the search words.

Examples:

In the previous exercise, you could key in: **train times + Milton Keynes Central**.

You are interested in finding information on football and in particular Arsenal. In the Search box, key in: **Football + Arsenal**.

You are interested in finding information about Oscars and Disney. In the Search box, key in: **Oscars + Disney**.

Using NOT

Use NOT or the minus sign when searching for information but omitting certain information.

Examples:

You are interested in finding information on football but not on Arsenal. In the Search box, key in: **Football - Arsenal**.

You are interested in finding information about Oscars but not Disney. In the Search box, key in: **Oscars - Disney**.

Using OR

You are interested in finding information about cameras. You could key in: **Camera OR photography**, since both of these might find useful information.

> ### Information
>
> For some search engines, quotation marks can be used to group words together (e.g. 'motor racing' may find more confined results than motor racing).

Try out some other searches with logical operators. Note the different search format requirements and which methods give the most relevant results.

19.11 Saving a web page as a file

Save one of the web pages you have visited as a file.

METHOD

1 Load the web page by keying in the address in the **Address** box.
2 From the **File** menu, select: **Save As**.
3 The Save As dialogue box is displayed.
4 Select the location where you want to save the web page and key in a filename.
5 In the **Save as type** section, select from the list (Figure 4.9).
6 Click on: **Save**.

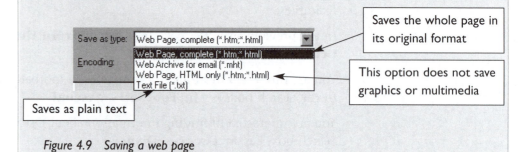

Saves the whole page in its original format

This option does not save graphics or multimedia

Saves as plain text

Figure 4.9   Saving a web page

19.12   Printing a web page

Modify page set up ready for printing.

METHOD

1 From the **File** menu, select: **Page Setup** (Figure 4.10).
2 Change the paper size, orientation and margins.
3 Use Internet Explorer Help if you want to set headers and footers.
4 Click on: **OK**.

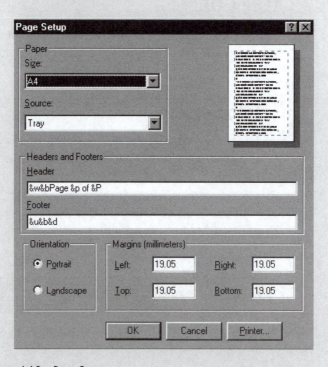

Figure 4.10   Page Setup

Printing

METHOD

1   From the **File** menu, select: **Print** or click on: the **Print** button.
2   The Print dialogue box is displayed (Figure 4.11).

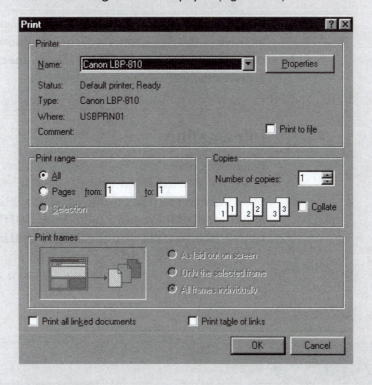

Figure 4.11   Printing

3   Make selections as appropriate.
4   If the web page is divided into frames, enter your choices in the **Print Frames** section.
5   Click on: **OK**.

Information

You can also choose to print a table of links. This is useful for reference.

WARNING: Remember anyone can set up a website and information may not always be correct or may be misleading. Try to check that information is from a reliable source.

METHOD

From the **File** menu, select: **Close**.

Note: Check that your computer has automatically disconnected from the Internet (is the connected icon still displayed on the **Taskbar**?). If it is, right-click on this icon and select: **Disconnect**. Forgetting to disconnect can prove expensive.

Information

Browsing offline

If you are worried about your phone bill, you can view and print previously accessed pages offline. To do this either load Internet Explorer and from the **File** menu, select: **Work Offline** or in the Dial-up Connection box, click on the: **Work Offline** button. Click on: the down arrow of the **Address** box to list previously viewed pages. Click on the one you want to view offline. (There is more about how to access pages offline in Task 20.)

Task 19) Check

Practice 19

Access the Internet and find the following information:

1   What events are on in Bristol this month? Pick three that might interest you. Print the details.
2   Three hotels in Bristol.
3   A road map of the route and average time taken to drive to Bristol from your region.
4   Does Bristol have an airport? If so where is it located? Print a map if available.

Task 20) Setting up favorites

When accessing the web it is well worth spending time setting up preferences. This not only makes things easier to locate but can also save connection costs. This task shows how to set up your home page (the opening page that is accessed when you launch Internet Explorer) and how to save page addresses you like so that it is quicker and easier to access them again.

When you have completed this task you will have learnt how to:
● change your browser's home page
● set up favorites.

20.1 Changing your web browser's home page

Change your web browser's home page so that it is the home page of 'This is London'. The address is http://www.thisislondon.co.uk

Information

Notice that the words *home page* appear twice in the sentence above. A home page can mean the page that your browser displays when it first starts up or it can mean the first page of a website. The home page of the 'This is London' website is the first page you see when you enter its address.

METHOD

1   Go to the 'This is London' home page by keying in its web address in the address bar.
2   The 'This is London' home page appears.
3   From the **Tools** menu, select: **Internet Options**. The Internet options box is displayed (Figure 4.12).
4   With the **General** tab selected, in the **Home Page** section, click on: **Use Current**.
5   Click on: **Apply** and then on: **OK**.

Figure 4.12   Setting a browser's home page

20.2 Saving a list of your favourite websites

Information

When you find a site that you would like to visit again, or a site that you visit often, it is a good idea to save the address of the site to make it easier to revisit in the future. These sites are then known as *Favorites*.

Save a site of your choice in your Favorites list.

METHOD

1   With the home page of the site displayed, from the **Favorites** menu, select: **Add to Favorites**.
2   The Add Favorite dialogue box is displayed.
3   A default name already appears in the **Name** box. Change the name if you want to.
4   Click on **OK**.

Accessing Favorites

METHOD

From the **Favorites** menu, click on: the website name.

Organising favorites

So that your list of favorites does not become unmanageable, you can organise it by creating folders to store similar content pages.

METHOD

1   From the **Favorites** menu, select: **Organize Favorites**.
2   The Organize Favorites dialogue box is displayed (Figure 4.13).
3   Click on: the **Create Folder** button.
4   Key in a name for the new folder and press: **Enter**.
5   Drag the relevant favorites into the folder.
6   Click on: **Close**.

Note: Use the **Move to Folder** button when moving multiple favorites.

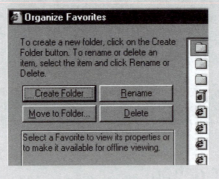

Figure 4.13   Organising favorites

Task 20   Check

Practice 20

1   Set up your browser to have a home page of your choice (if you do not have a preferred website there are some web addresses listed in this chapter).
2   Add some more websites to your favorites.

Sending and receiving email

This task shows how to send and receive emails.

> When you have completed this task you will have learnt how to:
> - load Outlook Express
> - create a new message
> - use a spellchecking tool (if available)
> - set message priority
> - send a message
> - receive messages
> - copy messages
> - reply to messages
> - print messages
> - close Outlook Express
> - use correct etiquette.

Note: Since Outlook Express can be configured to suit your specific needs, the Outlook Express settings used in the examples may differ slightly from your settings.

21.1 Opening Outlook Express

METHOD

From the **Start** menu, select: **Programs**, **Outlook Express** or click on the **Launch Outlook Express** icon on the **Taskbar**.

Either method will result in the Outlook Express window being displayed on screen (Figure 4.14).

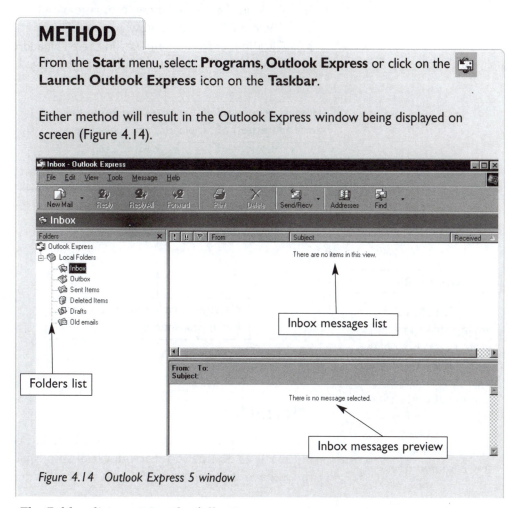

Figure 4.14 Outlook Express 5 window

The Folders list contains the following:

- **Inbox** folder – where incoming messages are stored.
- **Outbox** folder – where outgoing messages are stored.
- **Sent Items** folder – where sent messages are stored.
- **Deleted Items** folder – where deleted items are stored.
- **Drafts** folder – where draft messages are stored.

Create the message (shown below) and send it to someone you know who has an email address.

Note: If you do not have anyone to send it to, to practise, send it to your own email address.

Hello there [insert person's name]

I am learning how to use email. Please let me know if you have received this message.

Thanks.

[Insert your name]

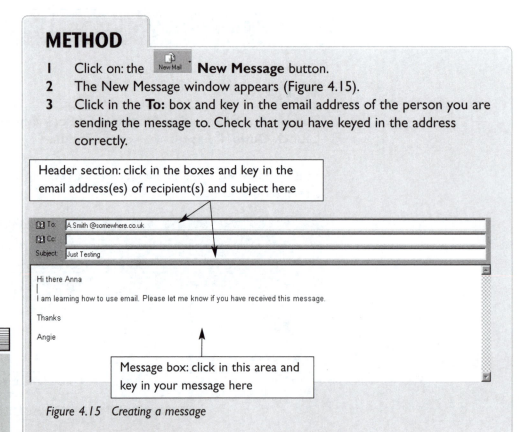

METHOD

1   Click on: the **New Mail** **New Message** button.
2   The New Message window appears (Figure 4.15).
3   Click in the **To:** box and key in the email address of the person you are sending the message to. Check that you have keyed in the address correctly.

Header section: click in the boxes and key in the email address(es) of recipient(s) and subject here

To: A.Smith @somewhere.co.uk
Cc:
Subject: Just Testing

Hi there Anna

I am learning how to use email. Please let me know if you have received this message.

Thanks

Angie

Message box: click in this area and key in your message here

Figure 4.15   Creating a message

Information

It is very important that the address is keyed in correctly, otherwise it will not reach its destination. Each dot (full stop, space and so on) is important. If you have made an error, you can delete it and key it in again.

Email addresses are made up of the user's name, followed by the @ symbol, followed by the address of the user's service provider. This includes the domain category; in Figure 4.15, co, meaning a company or commercial organisation in the UK, followed by the country, uk (United Kingdom). For example:

A.Smith@somewhere.co.uk

Common domain categories include the following:

ac = academic community (in the UK)
co = company or commercial organisation (in the UK)
com = company or commercial organisation
edu = educational institution
org = non-profit organisation
gov = local/central government
Each country has its own unique code – e.g. fr = France, ca = Canada, se = Sweden

4   Click in: the **Subject** box and key in: **Just testing**.
5   Click in: the **Message** box underneath and key in the message.

Note: The subject of your message 'Just testing' has replaced 'New Document' on the Title bar.

Information

Spellchecking
At this stage you can use: the button to check spelling.

Note: Spellchecking is not turned on by default. To turn it on so that spelling is checked automatically:

From the **Tools** menu, select: **Options**.
Click on: the **Spelling** tab.
Click in: the box **Always check spelling before sending**.

Setting message priority
Click on: the down arrow of the **Set Priority** button to determine the priority of the message. The default is Normal. A high-priority message has a red exclamation mark and a low-priority message has a down arrow.

6   Click on: the **Send** **Send** button.

Note: This will not send the message at this stage but will transfer it to the **Outbox** folder.

7   You are returned to the original Outlook Express window with the Outbox contents displayed (Figure 4.16).

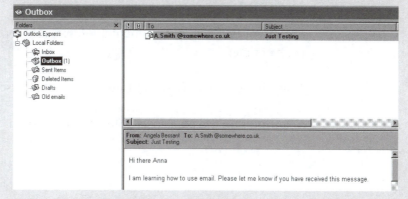

Figure 4.16   Outbox contents are displayed

Information

You have composed your message 'offline' – i.e. not connected to the phone line and therefore not incurred phone costs. When you have learnt how to use email, to reduce connection time it is a good idea to compose several messages and then send them all together. They will be stored in the **Outbox** folder until you are ready to send them. However, in this example for practice purposes there is just one message to send. Outlook Express will automatically check if you have received any incoming messages at the same time as sending your messages.

(21.3) Transmitting and receiving messages

METHOD

1 Click on the 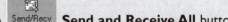 **Send and Receive All** button.
2 Outlook Express will send the message automatically and will display that it is sending the message.
3 When it has been transmitted, it is placed in the **Sent Items** folder. Click on the folder to check.

Information

Outlook Express can be set up to connect/disconnect automatically from the phone line. If this is not set you will need to do this manually and you should be prompted to do so. When you are connected to the phone line, an icon is placed on the Taskbar.

Click the right mouse button on this icon for a menu with the option to disconnect.

(21.4) Copying messages

The same message can be sent to more than one address at a time.

Sending the message on equal terms to more than one address

In the **To:** box, key in the email addresses and separate them with semicolons. For example:

A.Smith@somewhere.co.uk;J.Jones@somewhereelse.ac.uk

Note: You don't need a space after the semi-colon.

Sending 'carbon copies'

1   In the **To:** box, key in the first person's email address.
2   In the **Cc:** box, key in the second person's email address.

The main recipient(s) is the person in the To: box, with a 'carbon copy' sent to the second addressee(s).

Sending blind copies

Sometimes you may want to send a copy of the email to an addressee(s) without other recipients' knowledge:

1   From the **View** menu, select: **All Headers**.
2   A **Bcc** box appears where you can enter the recipient's address(es).

Note: With all the above, the message is again placed in the **Sent Items** folder and is treated as one message, even though it has been transmitted to more than one email address.

21.5   Opening received mail messages

Note: If you have not yet received replies to your emails then you will need to practise by sending an email to your own email address so that there is a message received.

METHOD

1   Load Outlook Express (if not already loaded).
2   You will notice that there is a number (in this example, 2) next to your **Inbox** folder, indicating that two messages have been received (Figure 4.17).

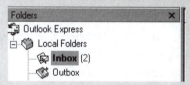

Figure 4.17   Messages have been received

3   The message(s) are displayed in the right-hand pane.
4   Click once on the message to see it in the Preview pane (bottom right), or double-click it to see it in a separate window (Figure 4.18).

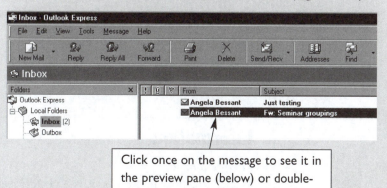

Click once on the message to see it in the preview pane (below) or double-click to see it in its own window

Figure 4.18   Viewing a received message

21.6 Replying to a message

METHOD

1   Click on: the [Reply] **Reply to Sender** button. The address and subject are already entered.
2   Key in your reply. *Note:* It is usual to key this in above the original message so that a 'thread' is formed – i.e. the sequence of messages is maintained.
3   However, if you want to delete the original message, select the text and press: **Delete**.
4   Send the message in the usual way.

Information

Click on the [Reply All] **Reply to All** button if you want to reply to multiple email addresses that were on the original message.

Click on the [Forward] **Forward** button to forward the message on to another email address(es). Key in the email address of the recipient(s). You can also add your own personal message to the new recipient(s) by clicking in the message window and keying in the text.

21.7 Printing messages

METHOD

1   Select the email in the Inbox or open the email in its own window.
2   Click on: the **Print** button *or,* from the **File** menu, select: **Print**.
3   The Print dialogue box is displayed.
4   Make any relevant selections.
5   Click on: **OK**.

21.8 Close Outlook Express

METHOD

From the **File** menu, select: **Exit** or click on: the **Close** button.

Information

Email etiquette
When composing emails, it is a good idea to follow some basic etiquette rules. These are be polite, brief and to the point and don't shout (i.e. do not use capital letters).

Task 21   Check

✓ Are you familiar with the following?

Sending an email	
Receiving an email	
Printing an email	

Task 22   Sending and receiving email attachments

In addition to sending text emails, you can send pictures and other types of files. This task shows how to send attachments to emails.

> When you have completed this task you will have learnt how to:
> * attach files to messages
> * receive, save, view and print attachments
> * delete attachments.

22.1   Attaching files to messages

Sometimes you may want to enclose something with your message (e.g. a picture or graph). In such cases you can add a file to your message. This is called an attachment. You can add more than one file. These then are called attachments.

Note: You will need to have a file to attach to your email. You can select any file that you have saved previously.

METHOD

I   Load Outlook Express, select new message and key in the following new message:

Hi [name of recipient]

I am practising sending and receiving attachments to email messages. Please find the attached file Stewart.

Please could you let me know that you have received this and also please could you send me an example attachment?

Thanks.

[Your name]

Do not click send yet.

---

2   Click on: the 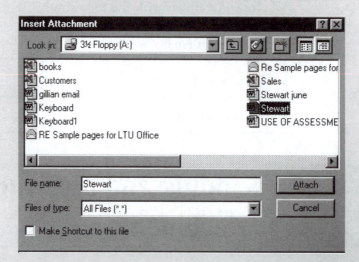 **Attach File** button.

3   The Insert Attachment dialogue box appears (Figure 4.19).

Figure 4.19   Insert Attachment dialogue box

4   Select the drive where the file is located (e.g. Drive A). Click on the file so that it appears in the **File name** box (or key in the filename).

5   Click on: **Attach**.

6   You will notice that your attachment is now shown in the header section (Figure 4.20).

Figure 4.20   Email with an attachment

7   You can now send the file in the normal way.

Information

You can attach more than one file to a message by repeating steps 3 to 6 for each extra file.

The time that it takes to transmit an email with an attachment(s) depends on the size of the attached file. Picture files are often very large so bear this in mind before sending whole batches of them! (The recipient also has to pay a connection fee when receiving.)

22.2   Viewing attachments

Note: If you do not have virus-checking facilities in place and you are in any doubt about the sender, delete the message and attachment. Click once on the message to select it, then press: **Delete**.

METHOD

Note: This is not recommended if you have any doubts about the sender's reliability.

When you receive a message with an attachment, the message has a paperclip icon next to it (Figure 4.21).

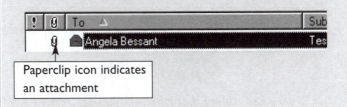

Paperclip icon indicates an attachment

Figure 4.21 Receiving attachments

1 Double-click on the message to view it in a separate window.
2 In the **Attach** box, double-click on the attached file (Figure 4.22). The file will appear in its own program window.

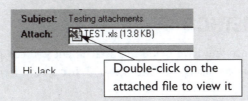

Double-click on the attached file to view it

Figure 4.22 Viewing an attachment

3 When you have finished viewing the file, close its window in the normal way. You are returned to Outlook Express.

Note: If the file does not open, it may mean that you do not have the suitable program to display the file on your computer.

(22.3) Saving a file attachment

METHOD

1 Double-click on the message with the attachment so that it appears in its own window.
2 From the **File** menu, select: **Save Attachments**.
3 The Save Attachments dialogue box is displayed (Figure 4.23).

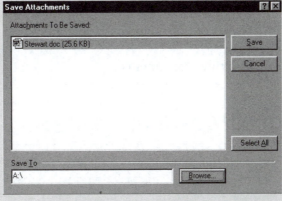

Figure 4.23 Saving attachments

4   Click on: **Browse** to choose where to save it.
5   Click on: **Save**

or

Right-click on the attachment and select: **Save As** (Figure 4.24).

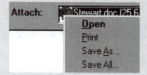

Figure 4.24   *Saving the attachments by right-clicking*

22.4   Printing an attachment

METHOD

Once you have saved the attachment you can print it from its application window using the **File** menu, **Print** or the **Print** button.

22.5   Deleting a file attachment from a message

METHOD

When sending attachments, if you have chosen the wrong one or need to delete one for any other reason, select the attachment by clicking on it. Press: **Delete**.

Task 22   Check

✓ Are you familiar with the following?

Attaching a file to an email	
Saving received email attachments	
Deleting attachments	

Task 23   Organising email

It is worth while organising your emails as you would with normal correspondence. This task demonstrates some methods for keeping things tidy.

When you have completed this task you will have learnt how to:
- ● delete messages
- ● sort messages
- ● move/copy messages
- ● search for a message

23.1 Deleting a mail message

METHOD

1   In the main window, select the message to delete. Press: **Delete**.
2   To select adjacent messages, hold down **Shift** when selecting.
3   To select non-adjacent messages, hold down **Ctrl** when selecting.

Information

Deleted messages are sent to the **Deleted Items** folder. It is a good idea to empty this folder from time to time to save space. To do this right-click on the folder and select: **Empty 'Deleted Items' Folder**.

23.2 Sorting messages

When you have numerous messages, you may want to sort them so that they are easier to locate. To sort by name, subject or date, click on the relevant heading at the top of the messages window (Figure 4.25). In Figure 4.25 there is a up arrow next to **Sent** indicating that the messages are sorted in ascending date order.

Up arrow indicates 'sent' is
in ascending order of date

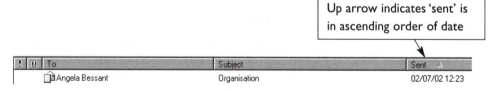

Figure 4.25   Sorting messages

For a more comprehensive sort, from the **View** menu, select: **Sort By**. Options available are shown in Figure 4.26.

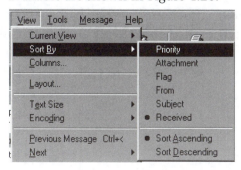

Figure 4.26   Sorting messages using the View menu

METHOD

1   Select the message(s) to move.
2   From the **Edit** menu, select: **Move to Folder** or **Copy to Folder**.
3   The Move or Copy dialogue box is displayed (Figure 4.27).

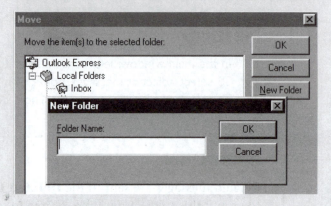

Figure 4.27   Moving messages to a new folder

4   Click on: **New Folder** and key in a name for the folder.
5   Click on: **OK**.
6   The message(s) is moved or copied to the new folder.

23.4   Searching for a message

METHOD

1   Select the folder where you think the message is saved.
2   From the **Edit** menu, select: **Find**, **Message** or click on: the **Find** button.
3   The Find Message dialogue box appears (Figure 4.28).

Information

In this example, the **Inbox folder** has been selected at step 1. This method searches the **Inbox** folder and its subfolders when the **Include subfolders** box is ticked. If you do not find your message in a particular folder, click on: **Browse** to select other possible locations.

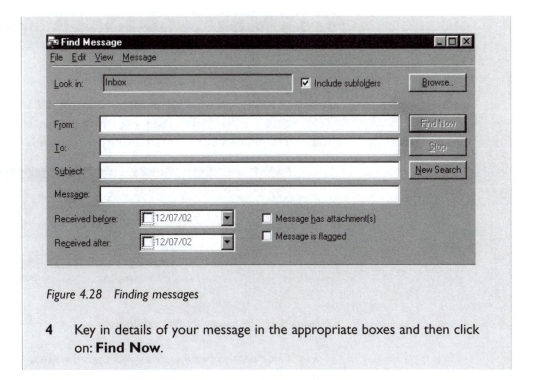

Figure 4.28 Finding messages

4 Key in details of your message in the appropriate boxes and then click on: **Find Now**.

Task 23 Check

Are you familiar with the following?

Deleting emails	
Sorting emails	
Moving/copying emails	
Searching for an email.	

Task 24 The Address Book

This task introduces the Address Book and how to organise it.

When you have completed this task you will have learnt how to:
- add a mail address to an address list
- update an address book for incoming mail
- delete a mail address from an address list.

24.1 About the Address Book

The Outlook Address Book enables you to store addresses that you often use. Using the Address Book means that you do not have to remember all those cumbersome email addresses and saves you having to key in addresses each time you send messages.

24.2 Adding an address to the Address Book

METHOD

1 Click on: the 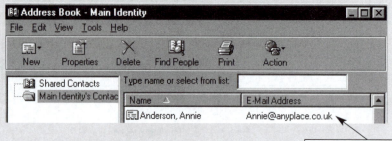 **Address Book** button.

2 The Address Book – Main Identity dialogue box is displayed (Figure 4.29).

Contact details list

Figure 4.29   Displaying the Address Book

3 Click on: the **New** button and then on: **New Contact**.

4 The Properties dialogue box is displayed (Figure 4.30).

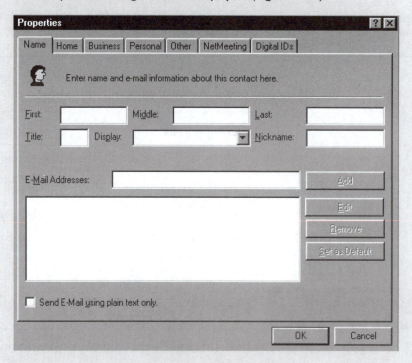

Figure 4.30   Properties dialogue box awaiting new contact details

5 With the **Name** tab selected, key in the details of your contact.

Note: By selecting other tabs you can enter further details of your contact as appropriate.

6 Click on: **OK**. The new contact is added to your Address Book list.

Information

Outlook Express can automatically add addresses to your Address Book when you send email. To set this option:

1   From the **Tools** menu, select: **Options**.
2   Click on: the **Send** tab.
3   Click next to **Automatically put people I reply to in my address book**.

Outlook Express can also add addresses to your Address Book by the following method:

1   Open the mail message from the contact.
2   From the **Tools** menu, select: **Add to Address Book** and click on: the contact name.
3   Click on: **OK**.

24.3   Deleting an address

METHOD

1   Open the Address Book as in 24.2.
2   Select the address to delete.
3   Press: **Delete**.
4   You will be asked to confirm the delete. Click on: **Yes**.

24.4   Sending messages using the Address Book

METHOD

1   Click on: the **New Message** button.
2   In the **Header** section, click in: the ⬛ To: **To:** box.
3   The Select Recipients dialogue box is displayed.
4   Click on: the recipient's name and click on: the ⬛ To: -> **To:** button.
5   Click on: **OK**.

Information

You can select as many recipients as you want and add them to the To, Cc or Bcc boxes.

Information

Viruses and the Address Book
In May 2000 the *Iloveyou* virus affected 10% of business computer systems in the UK alone and many more throughout the world, costing millions of pounds. It was spread via email. The reason the virus spread so quickly was because people rushed to click on the email attachment, it opened their address book and was then emailed to everyone listed.

Task 24) Check

✓ Are you familiar with the following?

Describing the Address Book	
Adding an address	
Deleting an address	
Using the Address Book when sending emails	

Task 25) Setting up an Internet email address

Previous email tasks in this chapter relate to using Outlook Express on your own computer. However, you can set up a web-based email address so that you can send and receive emails anywhere in the world using any computer attached to the Internet (e.g. in an Internet café or on a friend or relative's PC). Web-based email addresses are free and provide similar privacy to other email accounts. The only drawback is that you have to be online to write and read them. This tasks shows how to set up a web-based account.

When you have completed this task you will have learnt how to:
● set up a free web-based email address
● use a free web-based email address.

25.1) Setting up a free email address

There are many different free web-based email providers and they all have their pros and cons. Some of these include:

Hotmail   http://www.hotmail.com
Yahoo   http://www.yahoo.co.uk
Lycos   http://www.lycos.co.uk
Email   www.email.com

This example uses Hotmail. However you may find that for your particular requirements it is better to use one of the others.

METHOD

1   Load Internet Explorer.
2   Access the website http://www.hotmail.com (information is displayed about Hotmail together with frequently asked questions).
3   Click on: **Sign Up for a free Email Account**. A Registration page is then displayed.
4   Key in the information in the boxes. *Note:* You do not have to use real data but can use an alter ego. When selecting **United Kingdom** in the **Country/Region** box, you may have to wait for choices to be changed in the **Region** and **Postcode** boxes.

5   Read the terms and conditions and click on: **I Agree**.
6   If there are any problems with your completed form, the next screen displays this. Unfortunately most of the common email names have already been taken, so you may need to settle for something rather obscure. *Note:* Make a note of your email name and password.
7   You will be informed when registration is complete.
8   You are asked if you want any subscriptions you do not need to enter anything here but remember to click the box at the bottom to move on.
9   Finally you will arrive at the email page.

25.2   Working with web email

You will notice many things that are similar to Outlook Express email options. Therefore you should find it quite easy to use. If you get into difficulty, there is a good **Help** menu. Remember to logout when you have finished emailing.

When you next access the Hotmail website, you can enter your email name and password to login to your account.

Information

At the time of writing, you must use your Hotmail account at least once a month. You will need to check for any changes in terms and conditions.

Task 25   Check

 Are you familiar with the following?

The difference between web email and Outlook Express email	
Setting up and using a web email address	

Quick Reference Guide: Communication

Action	Keyboard	Mouse	Right-mouse menu	Menu
Access a website	Key in the web address in the address box			
Change View/ display				**Tools, Internet Options, General** and make selections from **View**
Exit Internet Explorer		Click: the ☒ **Close** button		**File, Close**
Favorites, add to			**Add to Favorites**	**Favorites, Add to Favorites**
open		Click: the **Favorites** button,	**Add to Favorites**	**Favorites, Add to Favorites**
Folder, create favorites folder		Click: the **Favorites** button Click: the **Organize** button		**Favorites, Organize Favorites**
Help	**F1**			**Help, Contents and Index**
Home page, set				**Tools, Internet Options, General** tab
Hyperlink, follow		Click: the hyperlink		
Images display do not display				**Tools, Internet Options, Multimedia, Show Pictures**
Load Internet Explorer	In Windows 98 desktop			
		Click: the **Launch Internet Explorer Browser** icon on the **Taskbar**		**Start, Programs, Internet Explorer**
Page setup				**File, Page Setup**
Print	**Ctrl + P**	Click: the **Print** button	Print	**File, Print**
Return to original page		Click: the **Back** button		
Save web page				**File, Save As**
Searching, using common logical operators	Use **Search** button or a Search Engine Use AND, +, &, or NOT, - , or use OR			

Quick Reference Guide: Electronic mail

Action	Keyboard	Mouse	Right-mouse menu	Menu
Access received messages		Click: **Inbox** in left-hand window Click: the message (to view in Preview) *or* Double-click: the message (to view in own window)		
Address Book, open		Click: the **Addresses** **Address Book** button		**T**ools, **A**ddress **B**ook
add address,	Open Address Book.			
		Click: the **New** **New** button,		**F**ile, New **C**ontact
	Click: the **Name** tab. Enter details. Click: **OK**			
delete address,	Open Address Book			
	Delete	Click: the **Delete** **Delete** button	**D**elete	File, Delete
Attach files to messages		Click: the **Attach File** button		**I**nsert, **F**ile
Attachment, delete	Double-click the message with the attachment so that it appears in its own window. Select attachment			
	Delete	Click: the **Delete** **Delete** button		
Attachments, save	Select the attachment			
			Save **A**s	**F**ile, S**a**ve Attachments
Copy/paste	**Ctrl + C** **Ctrl + V**			**E**dit, **C**opy **E**dit, **P**aste
Copy/move messages to folders			**C**opy to Folder Mov**e** to Folder	Edit, **M**ove to Folder Co**p**y to Folder
Create messages		Click: the **Compose Message** button		
Delete, message	Select message			
	Delete	Click: the **Delete** **Delete** button	**D**elete	Edit, **D**elete
Delete, text	Select text			
	Delete			
Exit Outlook Express		Click: the **Close** button		**F**ile, E**x**it
Folders, create new				**F**ile, **N**ew, **F**older

Action	Keyboard	Mouse	Right-mouse menu	Menu
Forward a message	**Ctrl + F**	Click: the **Forward** button	<u>F</u>orward	<u>M</u>essage, <u>F</u>orward
Help	**F1**			<u>H</u>elp, <u>C</u>ontents and Index
Load Outlook Express	In Windows 98 desktop			
		Click: the **Launch Outlook Express** icon on the Taskbar		**Start**, <u>P</u>rograms, **Outlook Express**
Print messages	(With transaction details and message visible in its own window)			
	Ctrl + P	Click: the **Print** button		<u>F</u>ile, <u>P</u>rint
Prioritise messages		With the message displayed, click: the **Priority** Set **Priority** button arrow		
Reply to all	**Ctrl + Shift +R**	Click: the **Reply All** Reply **All** button	**Reply to** <u>A</u>**ll**	
Reply to sender	**Ctrl +R**	Click: the **Reply** Reply button	**Reply to** <u>S</u>**ender**	
Route/address messages *Multiple recipients*	Key in the address in the **To:** box Separate addresses with semicolons (;) Use Cc box to send a 'carbon copy'. Use Bcc box to send a 'blind copy'			
Search for a message		Click: the **Find** Find button		<u>E</u>dit, <u>F</u>ind, <u>M</u>essage
Spellcheck	**F7**			<u>T</u>ools, <u>S</u>pelling
Transmit messages		Click: the **Send/Recv** Send **and Receive** button		<u>T</u>ools, <u>S</u>end and Receive
View attachments	(With message in its own window – attachment visible) Double-click: the attachment			

Useful Info

KEYBOARD SHORTCUTS FOR INTERNET EXPLORER

These can be very useful to reduce time online:

Alt + Home	Displays your home page
Esc	Stops download
Ctrl + D	Adds the current page to Favorites
Ctrl + N	Opens a new browser window (this is useful if you have a heavily hyperlinked page that you want to keep going back to to follow the links)
F5	Refreshes page
Ctrl + P	Prints the current page
Ctrl + S	Save the current page

Chapter (5) Managing files and folders

When you have created several files, you should start to think about storing them in a logical manner so that they are easy to find at a later date. It is also important to make backups (exact copies) of your files as a security measure should anything unexpected happen to your computer. The tasks in this chapter help you to clear up your clutter.

Task 26) Using Windows Explorer

This task contains practical exercises to facilitate working with Windows Explorer. Windows Explorer is an application that allows you to view and manage all the folders and files on your computer.

When you have completed this task you will have learnt how to:
- load Windows Explorer
- understand the computer's storage structure
- recognise folders and files
- create folders
- delete files/folders
- use the Recycle Bin
- close Windows Explorer.

26.1 Loading Windows Explorer

METHOD 1

From the **Start** menu, select: **Programs**, then: **Windows Explorer**.

METHOD 2

1 Right-click on: **Start**.
2 Select: **Explore** from the pop-up menu.

The **Exploring** window appears. In the example (Figure 5.1), $3\frac{1}{2}$ Floppy (A:) drive is selected in the left (Folders) pane and the contents of the disk in drive A are displayed in the pane on the right. Your window may not look the same since drive C may be selected. Do not be concerned about this.

Note: If your window has a different layout, you may be in **Web Page View**. From the **View** menu, select: as **Web Page** so that there is no tick next to it.

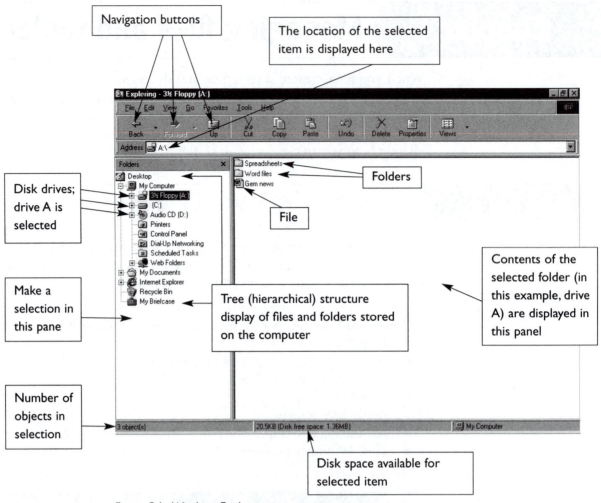

Figure 5.1 Windows Explorer

26.2 Computer storage structure

Examine your computer's storage structure. This is termed the *hierarchical* or tree structure because it branches off to different levels.

METHOD

I   With the Explorer window displayed, the **Folders** pane will have a similar content to that in Figure 5.2.

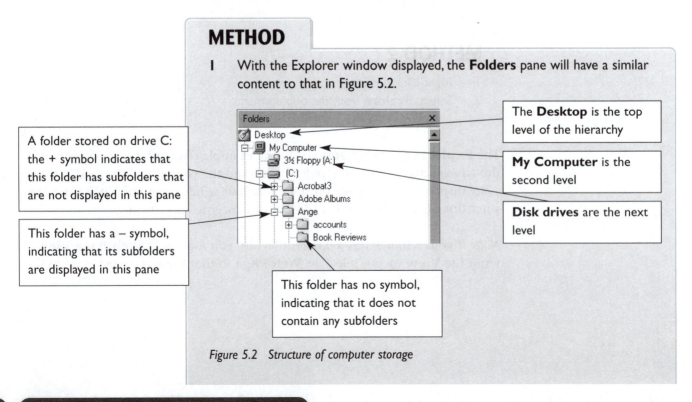

Figure 5.2   Structure of computer storage

> **2** Examine your computer's storage structure by clicking on the drives and folders to see what they contain or use the navigation toolbar buttons (shown in Figure 5.3.)
>
>
>
> *Figure 5.3 Navigation buttons*

Folders and files

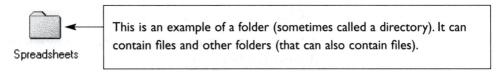

This is an example of a folder (sometimes called a directory). It can contain files and other folders (that can also contain files).

Note: The folder icon pops open when accessed.

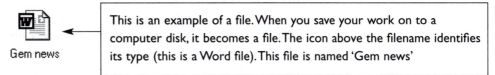

This is an example of a file. When you save your work on to a computer disk, it becomes a file. The icon above the filename identifies its type (this is a Word file). This file is named 'Gem news'

Displaying the contents of a folder

Double-click on: the folder.

> ### Information
>
> It is better to double-click the icon rather than the text as sometimes you will not get the action you expect (if you have not double-clicked properly). Instead a box may appear round the text, waiting for your input. If this happens, press: **Esc** and try again.

Creating a new folder

You can create new folders in which to store related documents. This is always good practice as it makes for easier location at a later date.

Example – to create a new folder on the disk in drive A:

1   First insert a floppy disk in drive A:
2   In the **Folders** (left-hand pane), click on: **3½ Floppy (A:)**.
3   The contents of the floppy disk in drive A are displayed in the right-hand pane.
4   Right-click in: the white space of this pane. A menu appears.
5   Select: **New** and then: **Folder**.
6   Key in the name for the new folder and press: **Enter**.

Creating a subfolder

You can create a folder inside the folder that you created above:

1   Double-click on the new folder. It is now displayed in the **Folders** pane.
2   Follow steps 4 to 6 above.

Information

You can create folders on the same level and also subfolders within subfolders, to suit your needs:

```
☐ Folder
  ☐ Folder A
    ☐ Subfolder
      ☐ subfolder within subfolder
  ☐ Folder B
```

Folder is the top level.
Folder A and Folder B are subfolders of Folder and are on the same level.
Subfolder is a subfolder of Folder A.
Subfolder has a subfolder contained in it.

Deleting a file/folder

1 Select the file/folder you want to delete by clicking on it.
2 Press: the **Delete** key.
3 You will be asked to confirm file delete.
4 Click on: **Yes**.

Note: When you delete a folder, its contents are also deleted so make sure you really mean to delete it!

26.3 The Recycle Bin

You can restore a deleted file (*not one deleted from a floppy disk*) from the **Recycle Bin** by clicking on: the Recycle Bin, selecting the file you want to restore and selecting: **Restore** from the **File** menu.

Emptying the Recycle Bin

It is a good idea to remove files from the Recycle Bin from time to time to save cluttering up the hard disk. To do this:

1   Click on: the **Recycle Bin** to select it.
2   From the **File** menu, select: **Empty Recycle Bin**.

26.4 Closing Windows Explorer

From the **File** menu, select: **Close**.

Task 26 Check

 Are you familiar with the following?

Loading Windows Explorer	
Recognising folders/files	
Understanding file/folder structure	
Creating a new folder/subfolder	
Deleting a file/folder	
Using the Recycle Bin	
Closing Windows Explorer	

This task takes you through some skills required to organise your files and folders. It also shows a quick method of finding a file or folder.

When you have completed this task you will have learnt how to:

- rename folders/files
- copy files
- move files/folders
- increase the number of recently used files in the applications' file menu
- recognise file types
- find a file/folder
- produce back ups

27.1 Renaming folders/files

METHOD

1 Right-click on the folder.
2 Select: **Rename** from the pop-up menu.
3 Key in the new name and press: **Enter**.

Information

Files can be renamed using the same method. Ensure that when renaming a file, if the file is displaying an extension, you remember to key in the file extension – i.e. the dot and letters after the actual name, e.g. fame.doc (in this case the .doc. This denotes that it is a Word file. There is more about file extensions later in this section).

27.2 Copying files

Note: There are several methods to copy files. Try each method. You can then decide which you prefer. Folders can be copied in the same way. When copying folders, everything inside the folder is copied too.

METHOD 1

1 Right-click on the file to copy.
2 Select: **Copy** from the pop-up menu.
3 Locate and right-click on the folder that you want to copy the file to.
4 From the pop-up menu, select: **Paste**.

METHOD 2

1 Select the file.
2 Hold down the left mouse and, at the same time, hold down the **Ctrl** key.
3 Drag the file to its new folder.
4 Release the **Ctrl** key and mouse.

METHOD 3

1 Select the file.
2 Hold down the *right* mouse button and drag the file to its new folder (it will become highlighted).
3 Release the mouse – a menu appears.
4 Click on: **Copy Here**.

Information

You can check that the file has been copied by clicking on the destination folder to reveal its contents. Method 1 is sometimes easier when you have numerous files and folders as these may scroll out of view when you are trying to drag them. Copy folders in the same way but substituting folder with destination.

27.3 Copying multiple files

METHOD

1 Select the files to copy.

Selecting adjacent files
a Select the first file in the group.
b Hold down the **Shift** key and select: the last file in the group.

Selecting non-adjacent files
a Select: the first file.
b Hold down the **Ctrl** key and select: each file in the group in turn.

2 Copy using one of the methods above.

27.4 Moving files/folders

METHOD

Files/folders can be moved using the methods shown in 27.2, except:

METHOD 1

At step 2, select: **Cut** instead of **Copy** from the pop-up menu.

METHOD 2

At step 2, do not hold down the **Ctrl** key.

27.5 Recognising file types

There are many different types of file depending which application they have been saved in (e.g. Word, Excel). It is useful to be able to recognise those that are most common. You can then decide which application you will need to open each file.

Right-clicking on a file and selecting: **Properties** displays its properties, as in the example shown in Figure 5.4.

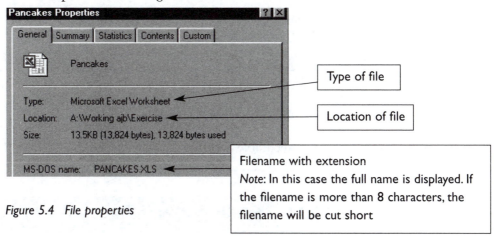

Figure 5.4 File properties

Information

When you save a file, the computer automatically gives it an extension – i.e. **a Word file** named **XXXX** becomes **XXXX.doc**. Other common file extensions are:

Extension	File type	Icon
.doc	Word	
.txt	Plain text	
.xls	Excel	
.htm	HTML, most commonly used on the world wide web	
.gif	graphics	

Information

You can also use the toolbar buttons in Explorer to view file properties. Select the folder/file, then click on: the **Properties** button. Alternatively, click on: the **Views** button down arrow and select: **Details** to view listed file details (Figure 5.5):

Figure 5.5   Views button

File details are displayed (Figure 5.6).

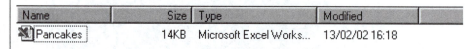

Figure 5.6   Details of file types

Executable applications such as Word and Excel have a .EXE extension.

27.6   Finding files/folders

If you are having trouble locating a file, use the following method:

METHOD

1   In Windows Explorer, select: **Find** from the **File** menu *or* from the **Start** button menu, select: **Find**, then **Files or Folders**.
2   The Find: All Files dialogue box appears (Figure 5.7).

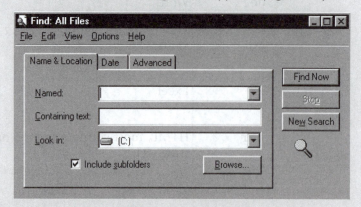

Figure 5.7   Finding files/folders

Information

If you do not know exactly what the filename is, key in just a part of the
name (e.g. **phone** will find telephone, phone list, headphones, etc). Use
the wildcard (a character used to represent unknown characters) – e.g. *.xls
to find all Excel files.

Information

Some file maintenance can also be carried out within applications, such as
Word and Excel.

27.7   Backing up

Backing up a disk means producing an exact copy of the contents of a disk.
This is done as a security measure in case anything happens to the original
disk. The backup should be kept in a safe and separate place.

Produce a backup of a floppy disk

METHOD

1   Select: $3\frac{1}{2}$ Floppy (A:).
2   Right-click; a menu appears.
3   Click on: **Copy Disk**.
4   Follow the instructions on screen.

27.8 Increasing the number of recently used files in the applications' File menu

When working in applications (e.g. Word, Excel), the **File** menu displays four recently accessed files near the bottom of the menu. Selecting the filename will open the file eliminating the need to access the **Open** dialogue box. You can increase this number as follows.

METHOD

1   Open Word.
2   From the **Tools** menu, select: **Options**.
3   Click on: the **General** tab.
4   In the **Recently used file list** section, key in the number of files you would like to see displayed.
5   Click on: **OK**.

Information

You can also backup your data by selecting **Programs**, **Accessories**, **System Tools**, **Backup** from the **Start** menu and then following the instructions given. You can back up selected files only by copying them to floppy disks (as Task 27).

If you have a CD drive you can write to, CD-recordable disks can be used for backups. They have the advantage that they can store considerably larger amounts of data than floppy disks and tend to be more robust.

Task 27 Check

✓ Are you familiar with the following?

Renaming files/folders	
Copying files/folders	
Moving files/folders	
Recognising common folder types	
Finding files/folders	
Backing up	
In applications, increase the the number of recently used files in the File menu	

Quick Reference Guide: Managing files and folders

Action	Keyboard	Mouse	Right-mouse menu	Menu
Backup a floppy disk			**Copy disk**	
Backup to floppy disk	**Start** menu, **Programs**, **Accessories**, **System Tools**, **Backup**			
Copy file/folder	Select the file/folder		**Copy**	**Edit, Copy**
	Ctrl + C	Click: the 📋 **Copy** button		
	Click where you want to copy the file/folder			
	Ctrl + V	Click: the 📋 **Paste** button	**Paste**	**Edit, Paste**
Create a new folder	Select where you want the new folder to be			
			New, Folder	**File, New, Folder**
Create a subfolder	Select the folder in which you want the subfolder to be and follow the steps for creating a new folder.			
Delete a file/folder	Select the file/folder			
	Delete		**Delete**	**File, Delete**
Display contents of folder		Double-click: the folder		
Exit Windows Explorer		Click: the ☒ **Close** button		**File, Close**
Find files/folders	**Start, Find, Files or Folders** or in Windows Explorer **File** menu, **Find**			
Load Windows Explorer	In Windows 98 desktop			
		Double-click: the **Windows Explorer** shortcut icon		**Start, Programs, Windows Explorer**
Move file/folder	Select the file **Ctrl + X**	Click: the ✂ **Cut** button	**Cut**	**Edit, Cut**
	Click where you want to move the file/folder to			
	Ctrl + V	Click: the 📋 **Paste** button	**Paste**	**Edit, Paste**
Recycle Bin, restore files	Double-click on the **Recycle Bin** icon Select the file you want to restore		**Restore**	**File, Restore**
Recycle Bin, empty			**Empty Recycle Bin**	
Rename file/folder			**Rename**	**File, Rename**

Action	Keyboard	Mouse	Right-mouse menu	Menu
Select files adjacent non-adjacent	Click: the first file Holding down: **Shift**, click: the last file Click: the first file Holding down: **Ctrl**, click: each file in turn			
View all file/ folder attributes		Click: the **Views** button arrow, **Details**		
View individual file/folder attributes	Select file/folder			
		Click: the **Properties** button	**P**roperties	**F**ile, **P**roperties

Chapter 6

Personalising your computer and saving time

There are numerous things you can do to make your computer exactly as you want it and save time into the bargain. Tasks 28 and 29 take you through the process of doing some of these things. Task 30 includes a table of Office shortcut keys.

Task 28 Screen savers, wallpaper, setting the clock

It is good fun to change the default settings on your computer from time to time. This task shows you how to give your desktop a 'makeover'.

When you have completed this task you will have learnt how to:
- set a screen saver
- set wallpaper.
- set date/time

28.1 What is a screen saver?

You can set a screen saver that activates when your computer is in use and you have not touched it for a while. Instead of the display showing what you are working on, it shows moving images on the screen. On older monitors, screen savers were originally intended to prolong the life of the screen by preventing 'burn in' of a permanent ghost image (caused by a long time static display). Newer monitors minimalise this risk but screen savers are still popular. They can act as a security measure when working in an open office (screen saver passwords can be set) so that your current work is not on view when your computer is unattended.

28.2 Setting a screen saver

METHOD

1. With Windows desktop displayed, right-click in a space anywhere on the desktop.
2. From the pop-up menu, select: **Active Desktop**, then **Customize my Desktop** (Figure 6.1).

Figure 6.1 Desktop pop-up menu

3   The Display Properties dialogue box is displayed.
4   Click on: the **Screen Saver** tab (Figure 6.2).

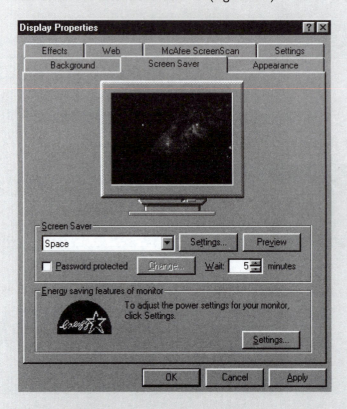

Figure 6.2   *Setting a screen saver*

5   In the **Screen Saver** box, click on the down arrow to reveal the
     screen saver options.
6   Click on an option and click on: **Preview** to see if you like it. Press: **Esc**
     to return to the Display Properties box.
7   Try other screen savers until you find one you like.
8   In the **Wait** box, select the time delay time between inactivity and the
     screen saver appearing.

     Note: You can password protect the screen saver so the screen saver
     will not deactivate until a password is entered. Remember to make a
     note of your password if you use this option!

9   Click on: **Apply**.

28.3   Setting wallpaper

Instead of displaying a plain-coloured background on the desktop you can
select a design. This is known as wallpaper.

METHOD

1   Access the Display Properties dialogue box as in 28.2.
2   Click on the: **Background** tab (Figure 6.3).

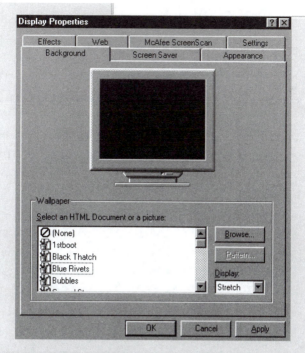

Figure 6.3   Setting wallpaper

3   In the **Wallpaper** box, scroll down and click on a design; a Preview is displayed on the screen above.

4   In the **Display** box, use the down arrow and select the type of display you require.

5   Click on: **Apply**, then on: **OK**.

Note: If you want to revert to the original background, select: **None** (top of list).

28.4   Setting date and time

The clock is normally displayed at the bottom right of the screen. If it does not show the correct time, adjust it as follows.

METHOD

1   Right-click on: the clock

2   From the pop-up menu, select: **Adjust Date/Time**.

3   The Date/Time Properties box is displayed (Figure 6.4).

Figure 6.4   Setting date/time

4   Make any necessary amendments.
5   Click on: **Apply**.

Task 29 Start menu and shortcut icons

To save time and effort trying to find your favourite programs and files, it is worth spending some time ensuring that everything is immediately to hand when the Windows desktop first appears. This task takes you through the processes involved.

When you have completed this task you will have learnt how to:
● add programs to the Start menu
● create shortcuts on the desktop
● arrange desktop icons.

29.1 Adding programs to the Start menu

As it is, the *Solitaire* program is rather long-winded to access, tucked away in a sub-sub-menu. If you play Solitaire a lot it is a good idea to add it to the **Start** menu, as in the following example. Other programs can be added in the same way.

Note: You cannot place any new programs below the **Programs** option on the **Start** menu.

METHOD

1   Open the sub-menus of the **Start** menu until you see **Solitaire** (i.e. **Start, Programs, Accessories, Games, Solitaire**).
2   Hold down the **Ctrl** key and the left mouse and drag **Solitaire** to the **Start** menu.

Information

You can remove programs from the **Start** menu by selecting: **Settings, Taskbar** and **Start Menu** from the **Start** menu.

29.2 Adding shortcut icons

Information

It is a good idea to create desktop shortcuts for applications that you use often. You can also create shortcuts for folders and files in the same way. This saves having to go through the **Start** menu. In this example we will create a shortcut for the on-screen calculator, **calc**. This is one of the *Accessories* applications that is part of Windows 98.

METHOD

1 From the **Start** menu, select: **Programs**, **Windows Explorer**.
2 The Exploring window appears.
3 Click on: the ⬜ **Restore** button (top right of screen) so that part of the desktop is visible.

   Note: A **Restore** button is displayed instead of the **Maximise** button when a window is already maximised.

4 Select the location of the application that you want to make a shortcut for. In this case, in the **Folders** section, double-click on: the **Windows** folder.
5 In the right-hand section, select: **Calc** (Figure 6.5).
6 Hold down the left mouse button and drag Calc on to the desktop. Release the mouse.
7 A shortcut icon appears on the desktop that looks like ⬜ .
8 Close the Exploring window.
9 You can now access and use the calculator by double-clicking on its shortcut icon.

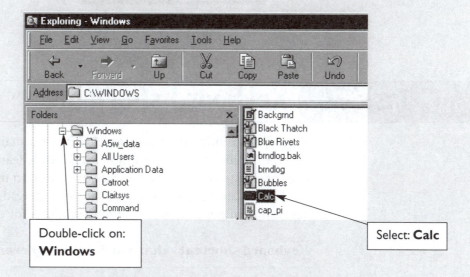

Figure 6.5 *The Exploring window*

Information

You can rename a shortcut by right-clicking on it and selecting: **Rename**. Key in a new name and press: **Enter**.

Note: Calc has not been renamed or moved from its original location within the Windows folder. You have only created a shortcut to access it in its original location.

29.3 Arranging desktop icons

If your desktop icons look untidy, you can tidy them up as follows.

METHOD

1. Right-click on the desktop; a pop-up menu appears (Figure 6.6).
2. Select: **Arrange Icons**.

Selecting **Auto Arrange** automatically lines up your icons. When AutoArrange is not selected, you can drag the icons to your preferred position on the desktop.

Figure 6.6   Arranging icons on the desktop

Task 30 Keyboard shortcuts

Although it is difficult to remember all the shortcut keys that you can use with Microsoft Office applications, it is worth while learning some of the most common, listed below. For this task, use Word to reproduce the table using all your newly acquired skills to make it look interesting, useful and decorative. You can then pin it up next to your computer for easy reference.

Keyboard shortcuts that work (almost) everywhere

Keyboard	Menu
F1	Help
F7	Tools, Spelling and Grammar
Ctrl + N	File, New
Ctrl + O	File, Open
Ctrl + S	File, Save
F12	File, Save As
Ctrl + W	File, Close
Ctrl + P	File, Print
Alt + F4	File, Exit
Ctrl + X	Edit, Cut
Ctrl + C	Edit, Copy
Ctrl + V	Edit, Paste
Ctrl + Z	Edit, Undo
Ctrl + A	Edit, Select All
Esc	Cancels items

Quick Reference Guide: Personalising your computer

Action	Keyboard	Mouse	Right-mouse menu	Menu
Date and Time, set	Right-click on the clock. Select: **Adjust Date/Time**			
Desktop icons, arrange	With the Windows desktop displayed, right-click. Select: **Arrange Icons**			
Screen saver, set	With the Windows desktop displayed, right-click. Select: **Active Desktop, Customize my Desktop, Screen Saver** tab			
Shortcut, create	In Windows Explorer			
		Drag object to desktop	**Create Shortcut**	**File, Create Shortcut**
Start menu, add items	Hold down the **Ctrl** key and drag the item to the **Start** menu			
Wallpaper, set	With the Windows desktop displayed, right-click. Select: **Active Desktop, Customize my Desktop, Background** tab			

Glossary

Application Another word for 'program' or 'application program'. An application enables you to do something specific (e.g. word processing)

Attachment A file that is transmitted with an email message

Backup An exact copy of file(s) used as a security measure

Browser A program that enables you to view web pages on the Internet

Bullets A small graphic (e.g. • used to emphasise and separate items in a list)

Button Using the mouse you click on a button to select an action. There are toolbar buttons, dialogue box buttons and so on

CD-ROM A removable storage medium that can hold large amounts of data

Clicking Pressing and releasing the left mouse button

Clip Art Artwork that is available for you to insert into documents

Cursor A symbol (which changes shape depending on what you are doing) on the screen showing where the next character will be displayed

Database A collection of information stored in an organised way so that it can be searched and sorted

Default settings Settings that are used unless you instruct otherwise

Desktop When Windows is loaded, the desktop is the work area that is displayed on screen

Desktop publishing (DTP) Creating integrated documents that incorporate text and graphics (e.g. newsletters, flyers)

Dialogue box A window that is displayed asking you for information

Disk storage device on a computer

Document A file containing text or pictures

Double-clicking Quickly pressing and releasing the left mouse button twice

Dragging Moving things around using the mouse

Drive The device that reads and writes on to disks. Usually: A: floppy disk drive, C: hard disk drive, D: CD drive

Email Electronic mail – messages that are sent and received on a network/on the Internet

File A unit of information stored on the computer (e.g. an Excel file)

File name + extensions The name given to a file. The extension is the letters after the filename that allow the computer to identify its type

Floppy disk(ette) A portable storage medium

Folder A storage location to keep related files together. Sometimes known as a 'directory'

Font A character set with predefined styles and sizes (e.g. Times New Roman)

Function keys The row of keys along the top of the keyboard (e.g. F1, F2)

Graphical user interface (GUI) A user-friendly graphic interface with the computer allowing you to communicate with it

Hard copy A printed copy

Hard disk Non-removable storage medium, usually housed inside the computer's system box

Hardware The parts of the computer system that you can see and touch (e.g. the monitor, keyboard)

Help Press F1 to access information on topics you are unsure of

Hover Place the mouse pointer over an object for a few seconds

Hyperlink A link (or hot spot) that, when clicked, allows you to jump to another location

Icon Small pictures that represent objects in a *graphical user interface* (GUI)

Internet A worldwide collection of computer networks

Internet service provider (ISP) A company that you can subscribe to be allocated an email address and to gain access to the Internet

Menu, drop-down and pop-up A menu is a list of commands grouped into related tasks from which you can choose. A drop-down (or pull-down) menu is displayed from the top of the screen downward when it is selected. A pop-up menu (usually activated using the right mouse button) pops up on screen

Menu bar A row of menu options

Modem A device that converts data from the computer into data that can be transmitted over the phone line and vice versa

Mouse A hand-held pointing device that is used to control a pointer on screen

Network Connecting several computers together so that they can share information and equipment (such as printers, scanners and so on)

Panes When a window is split into several parts, each part is called a pane

PC Personal computer, usually an IBM-compatible and not Apple Mac

Pointer The symbol on the screen that moves when you move the mouse or another pointing device

Powering up/booting up Switching your computer on and loading its operating system

Program A set of instructions that tell the computer what to do

RAM Random access memory. A temporary fast memory store whilst the computer is being used

Recycle Bin Deleted files are sent to the Recycle Bin. They can be recovered from here if necessary depending on the setup. Files deleted from floppy disks are not sent to the Recycle Bin

Right-click Click the right mouse button

Software The programs that make the computer work. Operating system software controls the *hardware* (see hardware) and runs the programs. Applications software includes Word and Excel

Scrollbar A horizontal or vertical strip that appears on the right or bottom of the window and lets you move through a document using the mouse to reveal previously hidden parts that couldn't fit in the window

Select To highlight a portion of text or an object on the screen so that you can manipulate it

Shut down Exiting Windows and turning off the computer

Spellcheck A command that compares the spelling in a document with that in the application's dictionary

Spreadsheet An application used for calculations and producing graphs

Subfolder A folder within a folder

Surfing An Internet term for following *hyperlinks*

Tab (in text) A preset position for aligning text

Taskbar A strip (usually) along the bottom of the Windows desktop containing the Start button, icons for all active tasks, quick launch icons and the system tray

Toolbar A line of buttons containing clickable short-cut icons

Undo A command that reverses your most recent action(s)

Virus A destructive piece of code that may damage your computer

Window A rectangular screen area in which applications are displayed

Word processor An application used to produce documents such as letters

Word wrap A word processing feature that automatically starts a new line when the text reaches the end of the current line

World wide web The visible part of the Internet containing linked HTML documents accessed through browsers. Often abbreviated to 'the web'

Appendix

Office Assistant

To hide the Office Assistant
Right-click: the Office Assistant, select: **Options** and set them to your preferences, click on: **OK**.

To turn the Office Assistant on
From the **Help** menu, select: **Show the Office Assistant**.

Checking spelling and grammar

There are many options available. Throughout the book documents are checked only *after* they have been keyed in, not on an ongoing basis. Should you wish to choose other options:

From the **Tools** menu, select: **Options**. Click on: the **Spelling & Grammar** tab. Select: your preferences and click on **OK**.

Use the spellchecker but do realise its limitations.

Changing the unit of measure

To change the unit of measure from inches to centimetres or vice versa:

1   From the **Tools** menu, select: **Options**, and then click on: the **General** tab.
2   In the **Measurement units** box, click on the down arrow and then on the option you want.
3   Click on: **OK**.

File maintenance within applications

In addition to using Windows Explorer, you can carry out file maintenance within applications. When opening or saving a file, you are able to gain access to your files within the dialogue box (shown overleaf). This is common to most Office programs. This box was opened in Word and displays only Word documents (by default). If you want to see other documents, click on the down arrow next to **Files of Type** and make your selection. Click on the **History** button to see recently opened files.

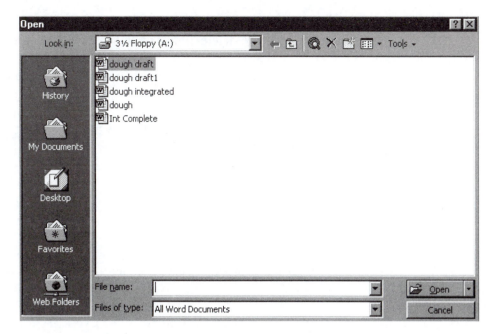

The main shortcut buttons that you will find useful are shown below. Using these will enable you to create folders and to find out details of your files.

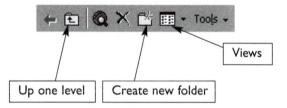

Up one level   Create new folder

Views

Clicking on the down arrow next to the **View** button produces a menu where you can select what detail you want to see in the **Open** box. The choices are: **List** (the default), **Details**, **Properties** and **Preview**.

Right-clicking on a file/folder will bring up the pop-up menu shown. This allows you to carry out any of the tasks on the menu.

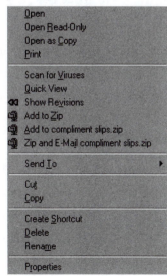

Deleting files/folders
A quick way to delete a file or folder is by selecting it and pressing: **Delete**.

Note: You cannot carry out file maintenance when a file is open.

A guide to document layout

When you have edited text or moved text within a document, remember adjustment of line spacing is often necessary. When proofreading pay particular attention to line spacing between paragraphs.

When inserting a sentence within a paragraph, make sure the spacing after any punctuation marks remains consistent. Make the necessary adjustments if required.

Line spacing between paragraphs
Press: the **Enter** key twice to leave one clear line space between paragraphs.

Underlining/underscoring
Underlining should not extend beyond the word. For example:

<u>word</u> is correct   <u>word </u>is incorrect

Punctuation

Be consistent with your spacing after punctuation marks. Use the following as a guide:

Punctuation	Mark	Number of spaces before/after
Comma	,	No space before – 1 space after
Semicolon	;	No space before – 1 space after
Colon	:	No space before – 1 or 2 spaces after
Full stop	.	No space before – 1 or 2 spaces after
Exclamation mark	!	No space before – 1 or 2 spaces after
Question mark	?	No space before – 1 or 2 spaces after

Hyphen
No space is left before or after a hyphen (e.g. dry-clean).

Dash
One space precedes and follows a dash – never place a dash at the left-hand margin when it is in the middle of a word or a sentence, always place it at the end of the previous line.

Brackets
No spaces are left between brackets and the word enclosed within them. For example (solely for the purposes of assignments).

Changing mouse properties

1   From the **Start** menu, select: **Settings**, **Control Panel**.

2   Double-click on: the **Mouse** icon.

3   The Mouse Properties box is displayed (see below).

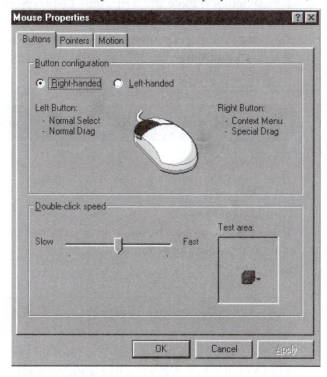

Changing to left-handed

Select: the **Buttons** tab and in the **Button configuration** section, click in: the **Left-handed** option button. Click on: **Apply**, then on: **OK**.

Changing mouse speed

Select: the **Motion** tab (see below). In the **Pointer speed** section, drag the slider to speed the mouse up or slow it down. Click on: **Apply**, then on: **OK**.

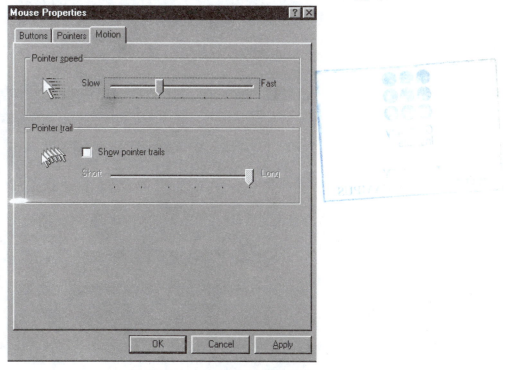

Printing Windows help topics

1   From the **Start** menu, select: **Help**.
2   When you have the help topic displayed (see Task 5), right-click in the pane where what you want to print is displayed.
3   From the pop-up menu, select: **Print**. The Print dialogue box is displayed.
4   Click on: **OK**.

Types of View in Word

Normal View
This allows for quick and easy text editing.

Print Layout View
This view allows you to see how objects will be positioned on the printed page. It shows margins and graphics.

When things go wrong

Life is life and sometimes things do not go as expected. For instance, if there is a power cut when you are using your computer, the documents and information that you have not saved to disk will be lost. It is important that you save your work regularly so that you will minimise the amount of effort required to re-do the work in such situations. Sometimes the computer may just crash (i.e. cease to function), either because there is a application error or a more serious system problem. If it is an application problem, restart the application. If it is a system problem, restart the computer by pressing the keys **Ctrl**, **Alt** and **Delete** at the same time. If this doesn't have any effect, as a last resort, turn the computer off and then restart it. Follow any instructions on screen.

When things go wrong don't be shy to ask for help